Also available from Conari Press

More Random Acts of Kindness
Kids' Random Acts of Kindness

Random
Acts
of
Kindness

The Editors of Conari Press

Foreword by
Daphne Rose Kingma

Introduction by
Dawna Markova, Ph.D.

Conari Press
Berkeley, CA

Printed in the United States of America on recycled paper

Cover: Sharon Smith Design; hand-lettering: Lilly Lee; illustration:
Pablo Haz

ISBN: 0-943233-43-7

Library of Congress Cataloging-in-Publication Data
Random acts of kindness / by the editors of Conari Press
      p. cm.
    ISBN 0-943233-44-5 : $8.95
    1. Kindness--Quotations, maxims, etc.   I. Conari Press.
BJ1533.K5R36 1993
177'.7--dc20
                                 92-38017
                                     CIP

For Anne Herbert,
the woman who started the movement

We would like to extend our boundless gratitude to those who shared their stories and suggestions:

Dawna Markova
Daphne Rose Kingma
Karen Bouris
Julie Bennett
Mary Jane Ryan
Will Glennon
Molli Nickell
Arthur Naiman
Tom Modic
Shirley Davalos
Tobias Stead
Pat Adler
Katherine Falk
Aaron Burack
Beth Nitzbey
Lewis Rambo

Robyn Brode
Martha Jackson
Nancy Evans
David Mack
Gail Derrin
Carol Brown
Bahman Sheikh-Ol-Eslami
Charlotte Burchard
Beverly Potter
Sebastian Orfali
Marilyn Chandler
John McEntyre
Donald McIlraith
Vanessa Carlisle
Roy Carlisle
Joan Edwards

Joel Drucker
Jane Goodwin
Ed Blonz
Marty Jacobs
Gary Rosenberg
Peris Gumz
Anne Powell
Dale LaPointe
Sheila Downes
Irene Imfeld
Tory Lee
Barbara Alexander
Adrienne Candy
Matthew & Ellen Cohen
Jerry Cimmet
Karen Shannon
Jane Seitel

Eric Mellencamp
Frances Wong
Damian Glennon
Alice Marie Alexander
Chris Sechley
Susanna Bluestein
Patricia Munson
Dina Huniu
Paula Gotch
Steve Worrell
Tami Cosgrove
Johnathan Peltham
Robert Bastian
Jane Dickson
Phu Nguyen
Peggy McQueen
Molly Fumia

To Become an Angel

*R*andom acts of kindness are those little sweet or grand lovely things we do for no reason except that, momentarily, the best of our humanity has sprung, exquisitely, into full bloom.

When you spontaneously give an old woman the bouquet of red carnations you had meant to take home to your own dinner table, when you give your lunch to the guitar-playing beggar who makes music at the corner between your two subway stops, when you anonymously put coins in someone else's parking meter because you see the red "Expired" medallion signalling to a meter maid—you are doing not what life requires of you, but what the best of your human soul invites you to do.

Most of us try hard to fulfill our obligations in life,

1

to be responsible parents, to reward and discipline our children, to assist our employees or colleagues, to support and comfort our spouses, to do our share of the work at the office and at home. But these deeds are what we're expected to do, what in fact we have agreed to do because of the mates we have chosen, the lives we have decided to live. They come, in effect, with the territory. To be reasonable, decent, civilized human beings who maintain the stability of our lives and our relationships, we must and we will do all these ordinary things.

But it is when we step outside the arena of our normal circumstances, when we move beyond the familiar emotional and circumstantial boundaries of our lives that our kindnesses, too, move beyond the routine and enter the realm of the extraordinary and exquisite. Instead of being responsible good deeds they become embodiments of compassion.

To become the perpetrator of random acts of kindness, then, is to become in some sense an angel. For it means you have moved beyond the limits of your daily human condition to touch wings with the divine.

No longer circumscribed by *can* and *must*, you have set

your soul free to give for the sheer, beautiful sake of true giving. In giving freely, purely, for no reason and every reason, you move into another person's emotional landscape—not because you must, not because you have no choice, but because in your heart, that majestically superhuman organ, the castle of your love, you have felt the spiritual necessity of acting out your love.

To become the person who behaves in this way is to be twice blessed. For, in enacting these beautiful, spontaneous, wholly gratuitous goodnesses, you transform not only the world, but yourself. The world—embattled, divided, discouraged, bone weary with its dog-eat-dog mentality—becomes newly laced with the sweetness of imaginatively unpremeditated love. Its atmosphere alters. Quietly, almost imperceptibly, because of the little kindnesses that have been unleashed upon it, it will begin to sing.

And you too will be changed. For in choosing to love not only those whom you have committed yourself to loving, but also those whose names, faces, and true circumstances you will never really know, you will be moved palpably, inescapably into understanding that loving and being loved is the one true human vocation. You will see yourself as an offering, generous, bountiful soul, as well as a needing human being. You will feel connected, centered, received—deeply bonded to the human stream. In giving love, you yourself will understand that we are held in the web of life—and delivered to our divine humanity—by the random acts of kindness, the love, that we give and receive.

Daphne Rose Kingma
Santa Barbara, CA

Living From the Heart

"Fear grows out of the things we think; it lives in our minds. Compassion grows out of the things we are, and lives in our hearts. "
-Barbara Garrison

 don't care what anyone else says. These are awful times. There is hardness in people's faces. Children wear bruises and forget to laugh. Everyone shrugs. People sleep under black plastic garbage bags and carry their world in a shopping cart. Despair and cynicism swirl around in our minds like discarded newspapers with headlines that say "compassion fatigue." Our souls are leaking. We are in a recession and we are receding. We are not moving toward anything. We are receding away. Away from what we are afraid of. Away from "not enough." Away from chaos. Away from poverty. Away from random acts of violence, from hurricanes and drive-by shootings and child abuse and homelessness and AIDS and drug wars. We are moving away from each other. But it doesn't have to be that way.

When I was quite small my immigrant Russian grandmother once told me that people in this country give from the wrong place. "When you give from here," she declared, pointing to her solar plexus and calling it some word that I could never pronounce, "it's like keeping a ledger book. I give you three so you give me three. I sweep the floor so you carry the bundles."

She pushed the wisps of white hair out of her eyes with the back of her red hands, shaking her head back and forth, *tssking* her tongue against her teeth. "That's not giving, that's trading. You give your soul away when you give like that. Giving is supposed to be from here," she said, pointing to the center of her chest with a feathery finger. "When you give from your heart, it's not to get anything back. There is no owing or owed. You just give because you want to give. When you give like this, it fills you up. It can't empty you.

"Your heart can never run out. The more you give

from there, the fuller it will be." Then she wiped her hands on the lemon yellow apron and pulled me to her. "It's like giving a hug. You remember this, *kitzaleh*. Remember to give from your heart. Even to strangers. When you give like this, there are no strangers. And remember to notice when other people give to you like this and be sure to say thank you."

Decades later, when I was struggling with a life-threatening disease, I traveled south to a conference in search of answers. One of the participants was a superb poet and writer named Maya Angelou. She spoke of surviving a childhood full of terror and violence. Her handholds through the darkness, she said, were countless acts of creativity by authors and artists. They were not trying to do something nice for her; they never even knew she existed. "Their work inspired me, shaped my thinking, exposed me to what could be possible," she recalled. "And I have never forgotten to say thank you for these random acts of kindness."

Without knowing it, without ever hearing my name or seeing the red knit dress I wore that day, Maya Angelou left fingerprints on my heart as if it were warm wax. I drove north perceiving the world through a different lens. Fate was just as unfair as it had been when I drove to the conference, but all I could think about, all I could notice, were the incredible gifts that had been bestowed on me every day of my life: the softness of a baby's cheek, Monet's *Water Lilies*, the ocean tides, the music of Tchaikovsky that swirled me round and round my bedroom until I was a sugarplum fairy, the songs of Johnny Mathis that taught me how to love, Mark Twain's writing that taught me how to be brave, Mrs. McLean's garden that taught me about beauty in the back streets of Brooklyn, a book by Natalie Goldberg that taught me how to find the voice inside which was yearning to write.

Each exit I passed on the interstate seemed to open another doorway to an embarrassment of riches I had forgotten to notice. The drive down to that conference had been fueled by my desire to "get": get healed, get love, get friends, get attention. My return trip was just that—a return to the lessons of giving from the heart that my grandmother had offered to me on a quiet morning long ago. A return to remembering that I was connected to the starlit sky, the fiery sun rising, the warm brown earth of Mrs. McLean's garden—if it could blossom every spring so could I! I remembered that I knew how to be enchanted by a story, dance naked in the early morning, sing at the top of my lungs in a hot shower, and rest easy in sunset silences. On that return trip home, my soul stopped leaking and my healing began.

Often in the workshops my husband, Andy, and I teach, we are helping people sort through vast amounts of pain and suffering. They are seeking ways to evolve beyond the crippling events of their histories, searching for ways to crumble the barriers behind which we all sometimes withdraw in defense and isolation. As part of that process, for the past two years we have been asking people to acknowledge to the waiting arms of their journals the handholds—the acts of kindness—in their lives. I talk for a while about the people and events that have rewarded me, not because I deserved them, but just because they came to me. Then I suggest a theme such as "Those who helped you learn to love" or "What has sustained you through hard times."

For twenty minutes or so, the madness and brittleness of the world begins to melt as people scrawl names, symbols, moments across the blank pages. Often some-one weeps. Afterward, as one person shares, another will nod his or her head, remembering a piece of music, a camp counselor, a man in a gas station, and add it to the page.

And then I ask people to pivot, to consider the random acts of kindness *they* have done. The room fills with silence as if it's holding its breath. Someone coughs, papers rustle. I watch in sadness as the clock ticks and people chew nervously on the ends of their pencils. One or two people will speak shyly as if they are giving a report to Mrs. Fitzgerald, the Girl Scout leader at the Merit Badge ceremony. I encourage and cajole until one woman admits that once she tied a string to all the bushes on her block, with a pack of Life Savers at the very end, a reward for anyone who was intrepid enough to follow her clue.

I don't believe this paralysis is due to compassion fatigue or a deficit of caring. I believe we are trained to notice *only* deficits, *only* where we are stuck, *only* how we are suffering. We are trained to believe that we don't matter and that we cannot make a difference. But we can. In one of our study groups, people secretly raised money to buy a new computer for a member who was yearning to write. He never knew who his benefactors were. In another, people anonymously raised money for a plane ticket to Ireland so that a man in the group could visit his homeland.

Giving in this way is as effective as an anti-depressant. It is salve for wild attacks of loneliness, fear, and despair. It reconfirms that each of us *does* belong, that we are all interconnected. It's a way of giving unabashedly from your heart without giving yourself away.

It is possible to decrease the suffering in the world by adding to the joy. It is possible to add to the light rather than trying to destroy the darkness.

Once you begin to acknowledge random acts of kindness—both the ones you have received and the ones you have given—you can no longer believe that what you do does not matter. It is as if you are dancing along a beach, making footprints on the edge where the shoreline meets the sea. No one is applauding. No one even sees your splendid gyrations of joy. You know full well that the tide will come and wash away the marks your dance has left. Still, the dance lives on in your heart, as does the simple, clean delight of being alive. As you are about to leave, you turn to face the shoreline one last time and you notice a small child, fitting his feet into your tracks, spinning, giggling. In that one moment, you know there is less suffering in the world. You know you do make a difference.

In a time when so many people feel unrecognized and unrewarded, when there are so many miserable things that happen to so many wonderful people, there are moments when you must stomp your feet in indignation and make room for the expression of your outrage. But you must also create space in your life for the expression of gratitude. What has sustained your soul? What has inspired you to hold on when all else was pulling you over a cliff? You are, we all are, the culmination of an infinite number of improbable gifts from myriad nameless sources.

A warning is in order here: Acknowledging the random acts of kindness in your life, be they in nature, works of art, moments of truth, rescue, or redemption, will bind you to them in a certain way. You will enter into an active relationship with them. Though they may not have been addressed directly to you, bringing them into your awareness can create a homeopathic response. The tough shell around your heart will begin to crack ever so slightly, and the circumference of who you are will swell full and ripe, aching to reach.

It is time for all of us to risk our significance. It is our hope as contributors to this book that you will become part of the lineage, that you will be inspired by what we have breathed into these pages, and most of all, that you will practice random acts of kindness, so that which came to you as seed will be passed on to the next as blossom, and that which came to you as blossom will go on as fruit.

Dawna Markova, Ph.D.
Burlington, VT

Random
Acts
of
Kindness

*E*very day I walk
down the mall to get a cup of
cappuccino, and every day I get
hit up for spare change. Every day.
The panhandlers all have these wonderful
stories but you never know what to believe.
After a while it gets to be an irritation, and then
I find myself getting upset that I'm so irritated over
what is really just spare change. One day this person
came up to me and said, "I just ran out of gas. My car is
about six blocks away from here I have two kids in the
car and I'm just trying to get back home."

The quality of mercy is not strained;
it dropeth as the gentle rain from heaven;
upon the place beneath; it is twice blessed;
it blesseth him that giveth and him that takes.
            -William Shakespeare

I said to myself, Here we go again, but for some reason I gave him $10. Then I went on and got my cappuccino. As I was walking back to my office, I again saw the man standing by his car, which had run out of gas right in front of my office. Seeing me, he came over and said, "Thank you, but I don't need the full ten," and handed me $2.

Now I find that being asked for money no longer bothers me and I give whatever I can every time I get the chance.

Agape is understanding, creative, redemptive goodwill toward all men. Agape is an overflowing love which seeks nothing in return. Theologians would say that it is the love of God operating in the human heart. When you rise to love on this level, you love all men not because you like them, not because their ways appeal to you, but you love them because God loves them.

-Martin Luther King, Jr.

17

$\mathcal{S}$everal years ago, when I was living in Chicago, I read in the newspaper about a little boy who had leukemia. Every time he was feeling discouraged or particularly sick, a package would arrive for him containing some little toy or book to cheer him up with a note saying the present was from the Magic Dragon. No one knew who it was. Eventually the boy died and his parents thought the Magic Dragon finally would come forth and reveal him or herself. But that never happened. After hearing the story, I resolved to become a Magic Dragon whenever I could and have had many occasions.

*"If there is any kindness
I can show, or any good thing I can do to any
fellow being, let me do it now, and not deter or neglect it,
as I shall not pass this way again."*
      -William Penn

When I was in college I attended a lecture one evening on hypnosis by a blind hypnotist. At the end of the session we did a prolonged relaxation exercise, and I walked out of the room with a completely different body than I had walked in with. It was a very powerful experience of actually feeling myself as a body for the first time in my life. As I was walking across a bridge on the way home from the lecture, a man jumped out of the bushes and tried to hit me. It was really strange—here was a random act of physical violence coupled with an incredibly powerful experience of kindness that had moved me into my body. The violence is now just a memory, but the hypnotic journey into my body forever changed how I feel.

"Complete possession is proved only by giving. All you are unable to give possesses you."
-Andre Gide

$\mathcal{M}$y husband and I were traveling in Italy with two small babies and an au pair. We would trade sightseeing time with the au pair so we could all visit the requisite churches and museums. But on this day we took the babies along, since we only had one day to go to Assisi and all of us urgently wanted to see it. The morning was wonderful—feeling like happy pilgrims, we read each other stories of St. Francis while the babies cooed and gurgled as we drove up the winding streets.

But by the end of a very hot day traipsing uphill and downhill in the 90-degree Italian sun, the two kids were crying nonstop. One was throwing up; the other had diarrhea. We were all irritable and exhausted, and we had a three-hour trip ahead of us to get back to Florence, where we were staying. Somewhere on the plains of Perugia we stopped at a little trattoria to have dinner. Embarrassed at our bedraggled state and

"My religion is very simple. My religion is kindness."
    -The Dalai Lama

our smelly, noisy children, we sheepishly tried to sneak into the dining room, hoping we could silence the children long enough to order before they threw us out. The proprietor took one look at us, muttered "You wait-a here," and went back to the kitchen. We thought perhaps we should leave right then, but before we could decide what to do, he reappeared with his wife and teenage daughter. Crossing the dining room beaming, the two women threw out their arms, cried, "Ah, bambini!" and took the children from our arms, motioning us to sit at a quiet corner table. For the duration of a long and hospitable dinner, they walked the babies back and forth in the back of the dining room, cooing, laughing, and singing them to sleep in gentle, musical, Italian. The proprietor even insisted we stay and have an extra glass of wine after the babies were asleep! Any parent who has reached the end of his or her rope with an infant will appreciate that God had indeed sent us angels that day.

"We do not remember days, we remember moments."
-*Casare Pavese*

Practice
Random Acts of Kindness!

☆ *Go to your child's class and talk about random acts of kindness. Then have the kids put together a booklet of the things they have done and those that have happened to them. Have them go home and teach parents the idea and come back to school the next day with stories from their families.*

☆ *Spend half an hour in a hospital emergency room and do one random act of kindness that presents itself.*

☆ *Offer to help people who could use the assistance to cross streets—seniors, the blind, small children . . .*

☆ *Plant a tree in your neighborhood.*

☆ The next time someone speaks to you, listen deeply without expecting anything.

☆ Find someone you've been close to and sit back to back with her. For a few minutes disclose the random acts of kindness she has done for you while she just listens. Then switch and listen to the wonderful things you have done.

☆ Yes, it's a drag, but why not put your shopping cart back in its appointed place in the parking lot?

☆ Write a note to the boss of someone who has helped you, thanking him or her for having such a great employee.

$\mathcal{W}$ho would ever think that a telephone answering machine could change your life? I had just broken up from a long and very painful relationship and found myself suddenly in a new city without friends, without anything to do or any desire to do anything. I was like a listless blob of expended energy. Every day I would come home from work and just stare at the walls, sometimes crying but mostly just sitting and wondering if this cloud would ever go away.

I had bought an answering machine—why, I don't know, since nobody ever called me. One night I came home and the red light was flashing. I couldn't believe it,

"Put your heart, mind, intellect and soul even to your smallest acts. This is the secret of success."
 -Swami Sivanada

a phone call. When I played it back, a wonderful male voice started to apologize—he had called the wrong number, and I burst into tears. But then he kept talking. He said my voice on the message had sounded so sad and he just wanted to tell me that it was OK to be sad, that being able to feel that sadness was important. His message went on for almost twenty minutes, just talking about how important it was to be able to go through the pain instead of running away from it, and how even though it probably seemed impossible now, things would get better. He never even said his name, but that message was, in a very important way, the beginning of my life.

"The purpose of life is a life of purpose."
-Robert Byrne

One night, while
my lover was inside our house
dying, I was on the porch smoking
a cigarette. We lived on a dead-end
street in a residential neighborhood that
had very little foot traffic. But that night a
woman walked by. I looked at her; she looked
at me. After she had almost passed the house, she
stopped, turned back, and walked up to the porch. She
told me that she had taken the bus from Fresno to find a
job, that she had left her children with someone, and if
she did not get back that night, she would lose her kids. I
called Greyhound and found out that the last bus to
Fresno had left. We went around about what she would
do. In the end I gave her $60 and she walked away. I did
not then, nor do I now, believe her story. But I felt it was
somehow important that I was being asked to give a gift
to a stranger when someone I loved was about to die.

"Do every act of your life
as if it were your last."
-Marcus Aurelius

I had a client who owed me a good deal of money. Eventually she stopped seeing me, but each month I would send her a bill and receive no response. Finally I wrote to her and said, "I don't know what difficulty has befallen you that you are unable to pay me, but whatever it is, I'm writing to tell you your debt is forgiven in full. My only request is that at some point in your life, when your circumstances have changed, you will pass this favor on to someone else."

"I am of the opinion that my life belongs to the community, and as long as I live, it is my privilege to do for it whatever I can. I want to be thoroughly used up when I die, for the harder I work, the more I live. Life is no 'brief candle' to me. It is a sort of splendid torch which I have got hold of for a moment, and I want to make it burn as brightly as possible before handing it on to future generations."
-George Bernard Shaw

was driving home from work on a crowded city street— parked cars on either side, traffic going about 25 miles per hour. I noticed a group of prepubescent boys on bikes, bobbing and weaving through traffic, being quite reckless and taking silly chances. Suddenly I realized that one of the boys was holding on to the door handle of my car, pedaling like mad to keep up. I honked and pulled over, gesturing for him to talk to me. First he took off, but then he circled back, looking sheepish and expecting a lecture, no doubt. His friends gathered around to see what would happen.

I got out of my car slowly, thinking about what kind of life this child must have to be willing to take such chances and wondering what I could possibly say that could make a difference. The words just tumbled out of my mouth. "I don't know you," I said quietly, "but I want you to live to a ripe old age with all your arms and legs intact." The boy looked at me, smiled, said "Thanks," and rode off. I don't know if I made a difference, but I pray I did.

When I graduated from college I took a job at an insurance company in this huge downtown office building. On my first day, I was escorted to this tiny cubicle surrounded by what seemed like thousands of other tiny cubicles, and put to work doing some meaningless thing. It was so terribly depressing I almost broke down crying. At lunch—after literally punching out on a time clock— all I could think about was how much I wanted to quit, but I couldn't because I desperately needed the money.

When I got back to my cubicle after lunch there was a beautiful bouquet of flowers sitting on my desk. For the whole first month I worked there flowers just kept arriving on my desk. I found out later that it had been a kind of spontaneous office project. A woman in the cubicle next to me brought in the first flowers to try to cheer me up, and then other people just began replenishing my vase. I ended up working there for two years, and many of my best, longest-lasting friendships grew out of that experience.

$\mathcal{T}$wo days before
my fiftieth birthday I had a heart
attack. It was a most surprising random
act of kindness. I had lived the previous
thirty years of my life as a powerful, successful,
and amazingly productive man. I had also lived so
cut off from my emotions that I couldn't even fathom
what the whole fuss about feelings was all about. I had
worn out the efforts of three good women, took pride in
my unfeeling logic, denied that there was anything
wrong or missing in my life, and was prepared to march
stubbornly forward.

Until I was felled and terrified by my own heart.
That experience unlocked a lifetime of buried emotions.
So, without knowing it, when the doctors revived me,
they delivered me to a life fuller and more beautiful than
I had ever imagined.

*"If you bring forth what
is inside of you, what you bring forth will save you. If you
don't bring forth what is inside of you, what you don't
bring forth will destroy you."*
    -Jesus

used to jog through the park every morning, and I always went by an old woman who sat on a bench with a small, very old, mangy dog. One day I noticed her dog wasn't with her. For some reason I stopped and asked her where he was. Suddenly, tears started running down the lines in her face and she told me he had died the night before. I sat and talked with her for over an hour. Every day after that we would greet each other as I came by; sometimes I would stop and talk with her for a while. She was very lonely but also very strong, and to this day I think of her when I'm sad, and it makes me smile.

"We cannot live only for ourselves. A thousand fibers connect us with our fellow men; and among those fibers, as sympathetic threads, our actions run as causes, and they come back to us as effects."
-Herman Melville

31

Practice
Random Acts of Kindness!

☆ *Buy a roll of brightly colored stickers and stick them on kids' shirts as you walk down the street.*

☆ *Make a list of things to do to bring more kindness into the world and have a friend make a list. Exchange lists and do one item per day for a month.*

☆ *Spend a week just being aware of things in nature that befriend you.*

☆ *Open the phone book and select a name at random and send that person a greeting card.*

☆ *Hold a random acts of kindness party where everyone tells the stories of kindnesses in their life.*

☆ *Walk around with a instamatic camera and take people's pictures and give them to them.*

☆ *Bring a little beauty into sterile places—drop off a geranium plant at a police station or a cutting from a houseplant to your local fire station.*

☆ *When someone is trying to merge into your lane in traffic, let him in—and why not smile and wave while doing it!*

☆ *All of you reading these words have loved someone, have done someone a kindness, have healed a wound, have taken on a challenge, have created something beautiful, and have enjoyed breathing the air of existence. Never doubt how precious, how vitally important you are. Every moment you make a difference. So, today, appreciate yourself as a random act of kindness.*

$\mathcal{I}$ moved into a
new house a few years back.
It was the first time I had a yard
of any size. There was a small lawn,
about thirty rosebushes, six camellias,
five rhododendrons, and numerous smaller
plants which, at the time, I could not even name.
I was a bit overwhelmed and not doing a very good
job of maintenance—especially of cutting the grass.

After a few weeks, I noticed—vaguely—that
something seemed different when I came home one
evening. But I didn't pay too much attention. Then one
day I came home to find freshly-cut grass, precisely
trimmed around the

"*I am done with great things and big plans, great institutions and big success. I am for those tiny, invisible loving human forces that work from individual to individual, creeping through the crannies of the world like so many rootlets, or like the capillary oozing of water, which, if given time, will rend the hardest monuments of pride.*"
-William James

edges, all around the sidewalks and driveway. I realized that someone had been weeding and pruning almost every day while I was away at work. Finally I caught the culprit in the act—my eighty-six-year-old neighbor, Mr. Okumoto. It's now been seven years and he's still doing it, not only my yard but the one behind his house and the one on the other side of his. He's now ninety-three and I don't know how long I'll be blessed with his diligent work. Maybe forever.

"People say that what we're all seeking is a meaning for life . . . . I think that what we're really seeking is an experience of being alive, so that our life experiences on the purely physical plane will have resonance within our innermost being and reality, so that we can actually feel the rapture of being alive."
-Joseph Campbell

I was driving home from work one day and the traffic was terrible. We were crawling along and out of nowhere this guy just pulls out onto the shoulder, passes a whole line of cars, and cuts me off so quickly I have to slam on the brakes to keep from crashing into him. I was really rattled. About fifteen minutes later, I'm stopped at a light and I look over and there is the same guy next to me, waving for me to roll down my window. I could feel my adrenaline starting to flow and all my defenses coming up, but for some reason I roll down the window, and he says, "I am terribly sorry. Sometimes when I get into my car I become such a jerk. I know this must seem stupid, but I am glad I could find you to apologize." Suddenly my whole body just relaxed and all the tension and frustration of the day, the traffic, life just dissipated in this wonderfully warm, unexpected embrace.

"Compassion is an alternate perception."
    -M. C. Richards

$\mathcal{W}$e had just searched a small village that had been suspected of harboring Viet Cong. We really tore the place up—it wasn't hard to do—but had found nothing. Just up the trail from the village we were ambushed. I got hit and don't remember anything more until I woke up with a very old Vietnamese woman leaning over me. Before I passed out again I remembered seeing her in the village we had just destroyed and I knew I was going to die. When I woke again, the hole in my left side had been cleaned and bandaged, and the woman was leaning over me again offering me a cup of warm tea. As I was drinking the tea and wondering why I was still alive, a helicopter landed nearby to take me back. The woman quietly got up and disappeared down the trail.

"What good will it do you to think, 'Oh, I have done evil, I have made many mistakes?' It requires no ghost to tell us that. Bring in the light, and the evil goes out in a moment."
-Vivekananda

It was a blustery day in Pasadena, California. The year was 1970. I had just started the second quarter of my first year in the seminary. Sitting in Greek class one evening I realized I had to quit; I had no heart for the study of classic languages and philosophical theology. The next morning, amid the protestations of the registrar and my adviser, I filled out the forms to drop out of graduate school. I had been doing very well and no one understood why I was leaving. But I felt increasingly clear about the rightness of the decision.

As I was walking between the registrar's office and the library, I passed the office of one of my professors. He was sitting at his desk, noticed my passing, and called me into his office. He wondered about the forms I was carrying and inquired about what I was doing. I

"I don't know what your destiny will be, but one thing I do know: the only ones among you who will be really happy are those who have sought and found how to serve."
      -Albert Schweitzer

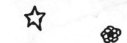

shared with him my decision to drop out and he very graciously responded with his disappointment and his blessing. Then he said something that eventually changed my life. Very kindly he remarked, "You are a talented young man with a future in theology, and even if you don't decide to go into the ministry, I think you should come back to complete your degree someday." I thanked him and walked out, quite touched by his kindness.

His prophecy came true. I returned two years later, completed my degree, found my way into theological publishing, and eventually the professor who had been so kind to me became one of my bestselling authors.

"Love is not getting, but giving. Not a wild dream of pleasure and a madness of desire—oh, no—love is not that! It is goodness and honor and peace and pure living—yes, love is that and it is the best thing in the world and the thing that lives the longest."
-Henry Van Dyke

I had been stuck for years in a place that refused to change. Everything seemed hard, solid, and unmovable. Making the most difficult and painful decision of my life, I left the woman I had shared my life with for fourteen years—and started an avalanche of change that forced me down a dark and anguished path of sadness and growth. Every time I thought I had reached the bottom, another trapdoor would open below me. I had spent almost a year jettisoning useless baggage until I felt stripped raw, empty-handed, and emotionally exhausted.

The one tangible thing I had done was to buy a new car—a nice one—a car that was soft and comfortable and responsive. I was sinking, but I was trying to find a way out. One night I woke up in a cold sweat from a devastating nightmare. In the dream everything had been taken from me. In the last scene I stood on a street corner watching my car being driven away, knowing that I had nothing left and no way to go on.

The next morning as I dressed
to go into San Francisco for a meeting,
I was filled with foreboding. The dream clung
to me and wouldn't let go. I arrived half an
hour early and found a parking place right in
front of the office I was visiting. It was a beautiful
fall morning and I decided to calm my nerves with a
walk. I was carefully locking my briefcase in the trunk
when I was approached by a very polite, elderly Chinese
man who was completely lost. I spread his map over the
trunk of my car, showed him where he was, and traced
the best route to his destination for him on the map.

He thanked me profusely and headed off. That
small exchange boosted my spirits considerably and
helped to dissipate the cloud of impending doom. First a
perfect parking place, then a simple but honest human
interaction. I put a dime in the parking meter and, after
registering my ten minutes, the dime fell out of the
empty cash-box hole and back into my hand; things
were definitely looking up. I returned from my walk
twenty minutes later and my car was gone. I reached in

41

my pocket but my keys were not
there—I had left them dangling from
the lock on the trunk. The day unfolded
like a bad dream. I called the police and they
came to the wrong address. When they finally
arrived I couldn't remember my license number (the
plates had only been on the car for a week). I got a ride
back home and spilled a full cup of coffee down my leg
and into my shoe.

My ride dropped me off at the home of the
woman I had left almost a year before. I had lent my old
car to a close mutual friend who was staying with her,
and I needed it back. I explained what had happened,
and the woman I had loved for fourteen years looked at
me and without a shred of compassion said, "Well,
there's a message from the gods!" It pierced my heart
like a knife. I knew she would regret having said it, but
that no longer mattered.

That evening I stood outside on the deck of my
house thinking about everything that was gone, everything that no longer mattered. Thinking that I never
imagined life could be this painful or this lonely. Thinking

how my self-support system had been reduced to driving my car, playing golf, and reading. And now my car was gone with my golf clubs and reading glasses safely locked in the trunk. I didn't know whether to laugh or cry so I did both. From behind me, inside the darkening house, I could hear music, Kate Bush singing the haunting refrain to Peter Gabriel's cry of despair: Don't give up . . . don't give up . . . . In front of me the sky bled a breathtaking deep purple-red sunset. I stood there watching the sunset dissolve into a stunningly beautiful and clear night. I knew that for all I had lost, I had lost nothing. That night I went to bed exhausted but at peace for the first time in many, many months. I was awakened at midnight by a night-shift dispatcher for the San Francisco police department. My car and everything in it had been recovered undamaged.

"Living the truth in your heart without compromise brings kindness into the world. Attempts at kindness that compromise your heart cause only sadness."
-Anonymous 18th century monk

$\mathcal{I}$ was at my sister's house, and I was there to rest. She lives in a big fancy house on the outskirts of Denver. All around her house is a canal. It's very safe, so I thought I would go for a little run—that's putting it too strongly—a little amble along the canal. I put on my little ambling shoes and started walking. All of a sudden, two women came running up the canal, screaming, "He's back there, he's back there, he's back there."

I have no idea why I did this, but I took one, two, three steps in the direction they were pointing and here comes this stark naked man with an erection running toward me. Without thinking, I let loose with an ear-piercing yell in the loudest voice I can, and he stops in

"What you deny to others will be denied to you, for the plain reason that you are always legislating for yourself; all your words and actions define the world you want to live in."
-Thaddeus Golas

mid-stride. I mean totally stops. Here I am, a woman standing there looking fiercely determined, and he stops, turns, and runs in the other direction. Then I went to the women who were still hysterical and helped them calm down. The man hadn't touched or hurt them. Finally I flagged down a trucker, and as the trucker called the police on his CB, I disappeared. I'm sure those two women were wondering, who was that masked woman?

"A human being is a part of the whole that we call the universe, a part limited in time and space. He experiences himself, his thoughts and feelings, as something separated from the rest—a kind of optical illusion of his consciousness. This illusion is a prison for us, restricting us to our personal desires and to affection for only the few people nearest us. Our task must be to free ourselves from this prison by widening our circle of compassion to embrace all living beings and all of nature."
-Albert Einstein

I was heading with my girlfriend through the Santa Cruz mountains on the way to a Samoyed breeder to pick up a new puppy. It was raining hard and the dirt road that was supposed to lead directly to the breeder's farmhouse was now simply a wide rut. My Honda was having more and more trouble with the mud and the steep incline, and there was an ugly drop into a now-rushing creek bed to one side of the road. Suddenly we ground to a complete stop: in the dark, stuck in heavy mud, with no tools, phones, or—so far as we knew—humans for miles.

We waited for about an hour, debating the merits of hiking in the pouring rain back toward civilization (miles away), trying to get the car unstuck (our attempts so far had just wedged us more firmly in the muck), and yelling (very, very loudly) for help. We were sitting in the car feeling hopeless when we saw faint lights behind us—we hadn't heard the engine because of the rain.

A young man in a VW stopped. He was headed

past us on the hill toward
his home beyond the breeder's
farm. He told us he had
towing equipment and would
come back and get us unstuck, and
would also let the breeder know we
were still on the way. We settled back to wait,
half doubting that he would return. After
all, it *was* pouring, it was now 10:30 at night,
and if he came back to do what he had promised, he'd
be completely covered in mud within minutes.
In forty-five minutes he was back with a truck
and towing equipment. Half an hour later we sat in a
warm kitchen, out of the rain, with hot cups of tea,
surrounded by teacup-sized Samoyeds.

*"Kindness is more important than wisdom, and the
recognition of this is the beginning of wisdom."*
-Theodore Isaac Rubin

During the Depression my grandmother was a society matron in Cleveland and, as she put it, "quite taken with myself." One morning she found a basket of food on her doorstep. It made her furious—how could anyone think that she was some poor needy person? Not knowing what to do, she put the basket in the kitchen without even bothering to unpack it. The next morning another basket of food was on her front step. By the end of the week she had five food baskets beginning to clutter up her immaculate kitchen, and she decided that the least she could do was to pass the food along to those who were really needy. The baskets continued to arrive for a couple more weeks, and my grandmother realized that she had begun to look forward to her part in helping find someone who needed them. When the morning deliveries finally stopped, she starting making her own food baskets to give away.

The moral of the story? Said my grandmother, "Someone knew I really was a poor needy person and found the best way possible to help me."

I live high in the hills and my body is getting old. One day I was out in my garden fussing with weeds and grew tired. I decided to lie back on the grass and rest like I used to when I was a small boy. I woke up some minutes later with a neighbor whom I had never met leaning over me, all out of breath, asking me if I were OK. He had looked out his window two blocks up the hill and saw me lying on my back on the grass, looking, I am sure, like the victim of a stroke or heart attack, and had run all the way down the hill to check on me. It was embarrassing but it was also so wonderfully touching. After we had it all sorted out, he let out a deep breath and lay down on the grass beside me. We both stayed there very quietly for a while and then he said, "Thank you for deciding to take your nap out on the lawn where I could see you. The sky is such a beautiful thing and I cannot remember the last time I really looked at it."

I have a friend who lives in a small village in Austria. She will be eighty next March. During the war her husband, a simple, uneducated Catholic farmer, decided he couldn't serve in Hitler's army because it would be an immoral act. My friend, Franziska, supported his decision even though they were desperately in love. Eventually, he was convicted of treason and condemned to death. The day before his execution, Franziska went to visit him for one last time in Brandenburg prison in Berlin. After watching him being cruelly hurled off a truck, hands and feet bound, she was led by two guards into a room with a long table and two

> *"A hundred times every day I remind myself that my inner and outer life depends on the labors of other men, living and dead, and that I must exert myself in order to give in the measure as I have received and am still receiving."*
> *-Albert Einstein*

chairs. As she and her husband began to sit across from each other, one of the guards moved the chairs so that when they were sitting, they would be barely able to reach their hands across the table and touch. After an unimaginable last conversation, it was time to part. The other guard offered to bring the prisoner out, and the heartless guard left. The second guard then turned away from the couple long enough for them to rush into a last embrace. Waiting until their sobs quieted somewhat, he then said quietly, "It's time to go." A token act of kindness for a Nazi soldier, perhaps, but that man gave them one more moment to experience an extraordinary love.

"If you help others, you will be helped, perhaps tomorrow, perhaps in one hundred years, but you will be helped. Nature must pay off the debt . . . . It is a mathematical law and all life is mathematics."
-Gurdjieff

$\mathcal{N}$ew York City
is a great place to find kindness
because it is always such a surprise.
I was going to a trade show and my
plane was delayed, so by the time I got
to my hotel everyone I was suppose to meet
had already left for the show. The concierge told
me that if I walked around the block I could catch
a shuttle. So I walked to the bus stop but the last shuttle
had already gone. Then a young man standing on the
sidewalk said, "The convention center isn't very far, it's
only four blocks." So I started walking. But it wasn't only
four blocks, and I walked and walked.

Suddenly it started getting dark, I was already an
hour late for my meeting, and I found myself in the

---

*"If someone comes to you asking for help, do not say in
refusal, 'Trust in God, HE will help.' Rather, act as if
there were no God, and no one to help except you."*
        -Zaddik

warehouse district, definitely
the kind of place you don't want
to be when you're all by yourself in
New York. Eventually I saw a little
light in the distance and started walking
toward it. As I walked, a taxi cab drove
past, then backed up and asked me where I
was going. I told him and he said, "Get in. I'll take
you there." By then I was really relieved, particularly
when it turned out to be quite far to the convention
center. To make the moment even sweeter, when the
driver dropped me off—safely back among my friends—
he wouldn't take any money from me.

"Some day, after we have mastered
the winds, the waves, the tides and gravity
we shall harness the energies of love.
Then, for the second time in the history of the world,
man will have discovered fire."
-Teilhard de Chardin

Practice
Random Acts of Kindness!

☆ *Write a letter of appreciation to that which in nature has been a safe place for you.*

☆ *As you go about your day, why not pick up the trash you find on the sidewalk?*

☆ *Write a card thanking a service person for his or her care and leave it with your tip. Be sure to include a very specific acknowledgment: "I appreciate the careful way you cleaned the room without disturbing my things"; "Your smile as you served me dinner really made my day."*

☆ *If you are in any of the helping professions, ask your clients to tell you their stories of random acts of kindness.*

☆ *For one week, act on every single thought of generosity that arises spontaneously in your heart and notice what happens as a consequence.*

☆ *A traveling salesman we know always carries cracked corn in his car and scatters it for birds during the snowy winter months.*

☆ *On Thanksgiving, call up everyone you know and ask them what they are thankful for so they can feel their own gratitude.*

☆ *Give another driver your parking spot.*

☆ *Talk to people at work about one of your random acts of kindness and ask what one of theirs is. Disclosure stimulates us to do more by emphasizing the pleasure of giving with no strings attached.*

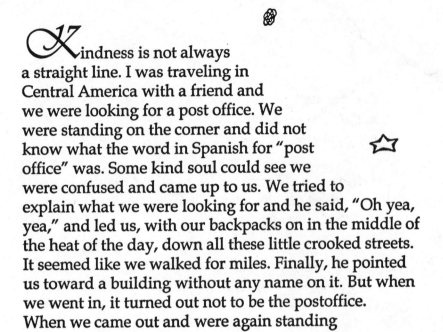

$\mathcal{K}$indness is not always a straight line. I was traveling in Central America with a friend and we were looking for a post office. We were standing on the corner and did not know what the word in Spanish for "post office" was. Some kind soul could see we were confused and came up to us. We tried to explain what we were looking for and he said, "Oh yea, yea," and led us, with our backpacks on in the middle of the heat of the day, down all these little crooked streets. It seemed like we walked for miles. Finally, he pointed us toward a building without any name on it. But when we went in, it turned out not to be the postoffice. When we came out and were again standing

"Let us not be satisfied with just giving money. Money is not enough, money can be got, but they need your hearts to love them. So, spread your love everywhere you go."
    -Mother Teresa

around looking lost,
someone else came up
and asked if she could help—
she knew where the post office
was. Again we headed off as she
guided us to another building which
also had no sign and which also turned
out not to be the post office. At this point we
decided that even though we didn't know where we
were, we were *not* going to listen to anybody else.
But then another person came up and said, "I can
help you." We said, "No thank you," but he was very
insistent. He actually grabbed me by the hand and
dragged me through the streets. Circling around, we
came back to the original corner where we had been
standing when we began. The stranger pointed across
the street and there was the post office.

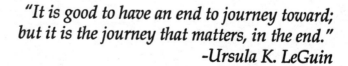

"It is good to have an end to journey toward;
but it is the journey that matters, in the end."
-Ursula K. LeGuin

When I was about 19 or 20, I was skiing down a mountain when I saw a women who had fallen. She was clearly hurt and crying and trying to get up, but she couldn't. So I flagged down somebody to get the ski patrol and stayed with her, talking to her, holding her hand, touching her shoulder. It was the last run of the day; it was getting really cold and snowing hard. About a half hour later, the ski patrol showed up and took her down the mountain. I stayed with her because she was so scared. She kept saying, "I think there might be something wrong." I said, "Well there might be. I'll make sure you get the care you need." Finally the ambulance came and took her to the hospital. I guess her leg was broken in about four places. I never saw her again, but it was clear my presence was important to her. I know that's true.

"To receive everything,
one must open one's hands and give."
        -Taisen Deshimaru

I used to make an eighty-mile drive to visit my parents. One forty-mile stretch of the road is in the middle of nowhere. One day as I was driving alone along this barren patch, I saw a family on the side of the road with a flat tire. Normally I do not stop in such situations, but for some reason I felt the need to do so that day. The family was very relieved when I volunteered to drive them to a gas station about ten miles down the road to get help. I left them at the station because the attendant said he would take them back to their car and drove on my way. About twelve miles later I had a blowout. Since I couldn't change the tire myself, I was stranded and not sure what to do. But in only about ten minutes along came a car and it pulled over to offer help. It was the same family I had stopped for earlier that day!

"This only is charity,
to do all, all that we can."
-John Donne

I was walking up Amsterdam Avenue in New York during a particularly dark time of my life. I had recently lost a lover, and the pressures of law school were gaining on me. The darkness in my heart must have come to the surface because as I walked by a destitute street person he turned to me and said, "It can't be that bad." Simple words that changed my life and brought the spirit back to my form.

"When we think we're separate, we lose power. Whenever I say 'my,' I have lost my power. Power is not my power . . . It is only gainable as part of a larger whole. Then you communicate with the rest of yourself—which may be a tree. You, reciprocally, are moved by the universe. Whenever you shut down connectedness, you get depressed . . . . It's fearful to know we're connected to everything in the universe, because then we're responsible."

       -Glenda Taylor

One day I was walking down the street and saw a small boy standing outside a video arcade, wistfully peering inside. I asked him if he needed a quarter and he nodded his head. His smile as I handed him the money was worth way more than twenty-five cents!

"The person who doesn't fit in with our notions of who is worthy of our love—the bag lady at the corner, the strange old man who rides through town on a three-wheel bike all strung up with flags—is just the person who, by not fitting into our patterns, insists that we expand not only our views but also our capacity to love.

"Today, see if you can stretch your heart and expand your love so that it touches not only those to whom you can give it easily, but also to those who need it so much."

-Daphne Rose Kingma

$\mathcal{A}$ few winters ago,
I was at a particularly distressing
dinner with a friend who was having
a difficult time with her then boyfriend
and was considering leaving him. I was
getting very worked up because the man she
was dating was a very close friend of mine and I
was torn between loyalty to her and my friendship
with him. She got so upset with me that while I was in
the bathroom, she paid her half of the check and left.

I was dumbfounded and hurt and so I rushed
outside in a weak attempt to reason with her. But she
was out of sight and I was so confused that I began to
walk without thinking toward the bus stop a few blocks

*"The mother who gives up her life for her children does
them no kindness but rather burdens them with the legacy
of a life unlived."*
    -Janet Falldron

away. I was so lost in my troubles that I started when I felt a hand on my shoulder. I whirled around and to my surprise, there was the waitress from the restaurant holding my purse and coat which I had left in the booth. Without a word, she handed me my belongings and gave me a hug. I burst into tears. She smiled and said, "I have been through that before, and I know how it is. Go home, take a hot bath, and watch *Casablanca* until you fall asleep." I laughed, thanked her, climbed onto the bus, and never saw her again.

"*If you live for love you spread kindness and compassion everywhere you go. When you stop believing in your heart you are but a sterile vessel wandering in the wilderness.*"
-Francis Hegmeyer

I was living in Chicago and going through what was a particularly cold winter both in my personal life and the outside temperature. One evening I was walking home from a bar where I had been drinking alone, feeling sorry for myself, when I saw a homeless man standing over an exhaust grate in front of a department store. He was wearing a filthy sport coat and approaching everyone who passed by for money.

I was too immersed in my own troubles to deal with him so I crossed the street. As I went by, I looked over and saw a businessman come out of the store and pull a ski parka out of a bag and hand it to the homeless man. For a moment both the man and I were frozen in time as the businessman turned and walked away. Then the man looked across the street at me. He shook his head slowly and I knew he was crying. It was the last time I have ever been able to disappear into my own sorrow.

$\mathcal{M}$y wife was dying of cancer. There were lots of nonrandom kindnesses in our lives. People who knew us did many ordinary and extraordinary things. But what touched many of us in our community happened early in my wife's struggle. We decided to have a water filtration system installed in our house to take the impurities out of the water. The plumber we contacted installed the system and wouldn't accept any payment. We found out later his father had died of cancer.

"There is a love like a small lamp, which goes out when the oil is consumed; or like a stream which dries up when it doesn't rain. But there is a love that is like a mighty spring gushing up out of the earth; it keeps flowing forever, and is inexhaustible."
-Isaac of Nineveh

$\mathcal{W}$hen I was
going through a very difficult
time, someone called me up and
played piano music for me on my
answering machine. It made me feel very
loved—and I never discovered
who had done it.

*"Every human being is
your counterpart. Every other human being possesses
and embodies aspects of yourself: your dreams, your
sorrows, your hope that your life will not turn out to be a
dirty joke. For each of us there was a time when the world
was young, a springtime of spirit that was later tested by
the winters of discontent; and in the midst of each of our
lives lies the haunting shadow of death. Therefore we are
all quite alike; indeed at the core we are all one, all lost—and
found—in the same mysterious enterprise that is life. Hold
this in your heart as you go about your day, and the world
will cease to be inhabited by strangers, and the burden of
life itself will no longer be a process of loneliness."*
    -Daphne Rose Kingma

had an older neighbor who was very kind to me, a father figure really. After he died, I noticed that his yard had become completely overgrown; his widow was not physically able to do the gardening. So one morning, after I saw her leave for the day, I jumped the fence and put in a few hours of work. It was my way of paying him back for the care he had taken of me.

"It is one of the most beautiful compensations of life that no man can sincerely try to help another without helping himself."
-Ralph Waldo Emerson

Practice
Random Acts of Kindness!

☆ *Your car is a place were you can make many courteous gestures with little effort. Sometimes smiling at the person in the car next to you or waving hello to a pedestrian in the crosswalk can really lift not only the other person's spirits, but your own.*

☆ *Visit a neighbor with a bouquet of flowers for no reason at all.*

☆ *Send a letter to a teacher you once had letting her know about the difference she made in your life.*

☆ *Buy a cold drink for your entire row at the baseball game.*

☆ Say "thank you" to someone who helps you and really mean it. You might want to look into his eyes, smile, and, if he is wearing a name tag, say his name as well.

☆ Ask an older person to tell you a story about his or her youth, such as what her favorite song was and why, or how he met his spouse.

☆ Let the person behind you in line at the grocery store go ahead of you.

☆ Order a mail-order gift, anonymously, for a friend or someone at work who needs to be cheered up.

☆ Take out an ad in your local weekly newspaper thanking a tree, a park, a stream, a sunset, for giving you comfort.

*I*t was on my
first trip to the States. I arrived
in New York as a student and went
down to the bus station to buy a ticket.
I had my money in one hand and my handbag
in the other—it didn't have anything valuable but
my address book in it. Going up to the counter to pay, I
put my bag down for a second and when I looked again,
it was gone. I couldn't believe it. I started to panic because I realized that without my address book I didn't
know how to get in contact with my brother, with whom
I was going to stay.

    The friend who was with me suggested we go to
the police. With what I knew about New York's reputation I told her that would be a waste of time. But we
went anyway and met two policemen who seemed to be
straight out of a television show. They couldn't have

*"The beginning and end
of Torah is performing acts of loving kindness."*
    -The Talmud

been nicer. They said, "Such a terrible thing to happen to you on your first trip to America." They took down the details and then started asking me questions, "Where was I going?" "Did I know how to get in touch with my brother?" Of course I didn't because my address book was gone. Then one policeman said, "Do you know anybody who knows him?" And I remembered I knew his in-laws. So they allowed me to make a long-distance phone call to the in-laws to get my brother's address and phone number. And when I got off the phone they said I should go ahead and call my brother right then and there so I wouldn't be anxious. Then they walked us back to the bus stop where we could find our way back to our hotel.

"The question is not whether we will die, but how we will live."
-Joan Borysenko

$\mathcal{I}$ am a corporate
lawyer, and several years ago I was
at my first closing. The investment banker
came to deliver a check for $55 million to my
client, and before my client arrived, I went to the
Xerox machine to copy the check for our records. I
put the check in the feeder of the copier, and it promptly
shredded it! I told the banker about the mutilated check,
and a moment later my client arrived, eager to receive
the money. The banker looked at me and said to the
client, "I can't believe it! I forgot the check!" He left and
returned an hour later with a new check, and I kept my job.

*"Our lives are fed by kind
words and gracious behavior. We are nourished by expressions like 'excuse me,' and other such simple courtesies. . .
Rudeness, the absence of the sacrament of consideration, is
but another mark that our time-is-money society is lacking
in spirituality, if not also in its enjoyment of life."*
        -Ed Hays

I had just quit a job I hated and was determined to find a way to live that felt right. Money was very tight and my car was dying on me—I mean really falling apart. A friend gave me the name of a guy who lived close to me and fixed cars. So I took my wreck to him and he fixed it. I mean he fixed *everything*—working on it for two days and charging me only $60. The parts alone had to have cost him quite a bit more than that! It was almost as though he read into my soul: "This girl doesn't have money, and she needs this car." He didn't know me from Adam. That car was my vehicle for getting to where I needed to go and this total stranger made that possible when I really needed it.

"Through our willingness to help others we can learn to be happy rather than depressed."
-Gerald Jampolsky

$\mathcal{M}$y husband and I travel a lot, and at the time this happened I had a horse, a wonderful horse. We were out of town when a one-hundred-mile endurance horse race (that's a race where people from all over New England get together and travel as fast as they can for one hundred miles) went right past our driveway. My horse, whose name was Dusty, decided that she wanted to join the race. So she jumped over the fence. Galloped off. No saddle. Nobody on her back.

The next day when my husband and I came home there was a note on the front door from the sheriff saying that my horse had gone back to the barn on the other side of town where she had been born eighteen years before. So we drove there. It was a lovely old farm, owned now by people I didn't know.

The new owners were a man, his wife, and their

"Give light, and the darkness will disappear of itself."
     -Erasmus

children, two little girls ages seven and five. And sure enough there in the corral behind the barn were the two girls and Dusty. The man told me that that morning when they had gotten up, the little girls had started screaming because at the top of the hill, with the sun rising behind her, was this beautiful palomino horse. They lured her into their corral and proceeded to spend the day brushing her and treating her a lot better than she had been for many years under my sometimes care.

They looked so happy. The seven-year-old girl turned and, with a trembling lip, said, "Can I ride her before you take her back?" I said that she could have her for another half hour or so. And then I went to the local general store and bought a bottle of apple cider. When I returned, they told me they had always wished for a horse but their parents really didn't have the money

"The heart that breaks open can contain the whole universe."
-Joanna Macy

for one. I sat them down
and told them I was going
to give them Dusty. And that
I wanted them to promise me that
someday when they were grown up
they each would find a little girl and
give her—a little girl they didn't know—some
very special gift that she had always wanted.

Then we celebrated with a bubbling glass of apple
cider, toasting to Dusty.

*"We who lived in concentration
camps can remember the men who walked through the
huts comforting others, giving away their last piece of
bread. They may have been few in number, but they offer
sufficient proof that everything can be taken away from a
man but one thing: the last of the human freedoms—to
choose one's attitude in any given set of circumstances, to
choose one's own way."*
-Viktor Frankl

When I was in high school, I started playing field hockey. Since this was on the West Coast, there were no organized men's leagues, and we would more often than not end up playing college teams or adult club teams. One day we played the local university team which included one of the best field hockey players in the country. They killed us. I remember running around like mad, exerting massive amounts of energy while this one guy just glided around, past, and through us to score whenever he wanted. After the game I was sitting on the ground trying to catch my breath when the star walked over and started talking to me. For a while he just talked, going into all the intricacies of the game; he spoke to me as if I were an equal, as if I already understood all the things he was saying. After I had finally caught my breath, he took me back out on the field and spent an hour showing me various moves and tactics. I know it sounds silly, but even though the words were all about field hockey, the feeling it gave me was so much larger.

$\mathscr{I}$ was in Tokyo,
at the main train station, trying
to take the bullet train to Kyoto.
The station is huge—there's more
than fifty departure and arrival platforms
and all the signs are in Japanese. No one I
tried to get directions from spoke any English.
The time I was supposed to depart was nearing
and I had not yet found the correct platform. In a
state of near panic, I went to a ticket window and
explained my predicament to the agent, only to be met
with his blank stare. Obviously, he spoke no English.

Pointing to my tickets and to my suitcases, I
communicated my desperation to him in body language.

*"Experience praises the most
happy the one who made the most people happy."*
   -Karl Marx

Suddenly, his face showed
signs of comprehension. Jumping
across the counter, he grabbed one
of my suitcases with one hand and my
arm with the other and began to run. For
the next five minutes or so, the ticket agent
and I were engaged in a weird dance as we weaved
across platforms, bridges, and alleys, through tunnels,
and past crowded passages, suitcases in hand, to the one
platform he knew was the right one. Literally seconds
after I entered the car into which he pushed me and
shoved the suitcases, the door closed and the train pulled
out of the station.

*"Keep on sowing your seed,
for you never know which will grow—perhaps it all will."*
-Ecclesiastes

*O*n the summer
of 1977, a friend and I were
driving in my 1967 VW bug
to Ashland, Oregon, when my car
threw a rod in the middle of nowhere
on a Sunday (of course). We finally tracked
down a tow truck driver who took the car to
some swampy, willowy grove by the ocean—a
wonderful place of rest, a kind of car heaven.

Meanwhile, however, we were completely stuck
in this godforsaken place, at least until some means of
transportation could be found when businesses opened
up again on Monday. So the tow truck driver took us to
his wonderful little woodsy home in the Mendocino mountains, fed us, and put us up for the night. Wonderful!

---

*"Each small task of everyday
life is part of the total harmony of the universe."*
-St. Theresa of Lisieux

For years, the Oakland, California, neighbors watched as Mary's house and yard slowly decayed. Mary was an elderly, wheelchair-bound widow who could no longer manage the necessary repairs and maintenance on her house. One day a couple of neighbors—a bus driver and an auto worker—went down to the city's Office of Community Development, got forty-five gallons of Mary's favorite-colored paint and a handful of painting supplies, and set to work. By the time they had finished, they had also put in a new lawn, cut back the tangled shrubs, and topped off the paint job with eye-catching trim.

"Little kindnesses . . . will broaden your heart, and slowly you will habituate yourself to helping your fellow man in many ways."
-Zadik

I was traveling
by Britrail through England
and Scotland and got caught on
a weekend with no money. (I had
a bank account but couldn't get any
cash out until Monday.) I decided to
ride an overnight train from London to
Inverness on Sunday so I wouldn't have to
worry about staying in a hotel; the next morning
I could go to the bank and all would be fine. I didn't
check the rail schedule very well, though, and the train I
was on came to a dead end in Glasgow at one a.m.

At the time, Glasgow had a terribly rough reputation. I'd never been there and never wanted to be, but there I was with no money and nowhere to go. For some reason (exhaustion? innocence?), instead of just staying on a bench in the train station till morning, I picked up all my bags and started walking down the streets of Glasgow.

"It is in the shelter of each other that the people live."
    -Irish proverb

The story could have ended pretty badly. There were gangs of what looked like thugs on every corner, and here was I, a twenty-something, American woman who obviously had nowhere to go. But then a policeman came along. He took me to a nearby YWCA, talked the matron into letting me stay (it was a shelter for battered wives and didn't really take in tourists), and even paid the fee when I told him I didn't have any money! The next morning, I went to the bank, walked to the police station, and left it for him. I'm sure he was surprised to get it, since he obviously thought I didn't really have any money. The kindness of that policeman and also the women in the shelter who gave me breakfast and let me take a shower and wash my clothes made me think Glasgow was a very friendly place!

"Our deeds determine us, as much as we determine our deeds."
-George Eliot

$\mathcal{W}$e were traveling
in Prague, one of the most confusing
cities in Europe. It was nighttime and we
were in a large rented car, utterly lost, finding
our considerable German, moderate French, and
hopeful English unusable on any storekeeper or street-
corner policeman. The street signs were all painted on
dark brown metal and averaged about fifteen letters, all
consonants. At one point we found ourselves at the end
of a dead end—Czech mate!

Finally we found ourselves in the middle of a
pedestrian mall with nowhere to go, wondering if we

*"Love and pity and wish
well to every soul in the world;
dwell in love, and then you dwell in God; hate nothing but
the evil that stirs in your own heart."*
    -William Law

should just pull over
and spend the night in the
car. A man and his wife appeared.
We tried German once more and this
time it worked. We asked directions to
Wenceslaus Platz. He started explaining at length
until his wife pulled at his sleeve and said, "You can't get
there from here. Get in and show them." So he got in our
car, she in theirs, and they accompanied us through a
considerable section of Prague to the door of our hotel, at
which point they wished us a cordial good-night. We
never saw them again, but were safe in a strange city
thanks to the kindness of strangers.

*"Whenever you are to do a
thing, though it can never be known but to yourself, ask
yourself how you would act were all the world looking at
you and act accordingly."*
-Thomas Jefferson

$\mathcal{M}$y grandmother
was born in Russia at a time of
great confusion and instability. She
emigrated to this country as a young
girl and ended up marrying a man who
was extraordinarily successful. She could
have lived in the fanciest neighborhood and
eaten only at the best restaurants; instead she
lived in a very modest area and would go to
Woolworth's for coffee. In those days, a cup of coffee cost
five cents, and whenever my grandmother would buy a
cup, she would always leave a five dollar tip. Her expla-
nation was simple: "They work hard for their money."

---

*"True kindness presupposed
the faculty of imagining as one's own the suffering and
joy of others."*
        -Andre Gide

I was about to go into the hospital to be operated on for breast cancer when there was a knock on my door. It was a man from the utility company telling me that the next week they were going to tear up the street in front of my house to put in a new sewer. My face fell and I said, "This is terrible! I'll just be back from the hospital convalescing from cancer surgery." The man turned and left. I later found out that they totally rearranged their schedule so that the work on my street wouldn't begin till several weeks later to give me some peace and quiet when I first got home! For years later, I would see that guy working on the sewers around town and we'd wave to one another.

"Tenderness and kindness are not signs of weakness and despair but manifestations of strength and resolution."
-Kahil Gibran

The other day I went with a friend to the grocery store to buy a few things, and we were standing in the express line which, as usual, was about a block long. In front of us was a woman with a gallon of milk and a loaf of bread who was muttering under her breath about how disgraceful it was that she had to wait so long, how the store never had enough checkers, how express was supposed to mean fast, how the clerk wasn't supposed to let people use checks and she could see him cashing a check for some idiot who couldn't even read the sign—it was a constant monologue all the way up to the checkstand.

When she finally arrived, the clerk rang up her total as just over $4; reaching into her purse, she discovered she had no money. She just stopped dead with an incredulous expression on her face. I was just standing there transfixed when my friend reached over, handed the clerk a $5 bill, and said, "I'll pay for it." I hope the incident makes her future waits a little easier to endure.

$\mathcal{I}$'m a doctor. Every day I come into the office and, probably like most doctors, slip into my professional caring role. I try hard to always be in a positive and attentive frame of mind for each and every one of my patients. But every now and then one of my patients will turn the tables on me and it is always such a genuinely touching thing. There I am, figuratively leaning forward, ready to be the one to do the giving, and out comes a bag of vegetables fresh from the garden, a coffee cake, a bouquet of home-grown flowers. The turn-around—the receiver giving to the giver—never fails to take me by surprise and always puts a large goofy grin on my face.

"Kind words can be short and easy to speak but their echoes are truly endless."
-Mother Teresa

Practice
Random Acts of Kindness!

☆ *Buy a big box of donuts or chocolates for the office next to yours. Or the kids who hang out on the street corner. Or the UPS person or the mail carrier.*

☆ *Make an anonymous donation to some local charity that is actively helping people—feeding the homeless, providing foster care for children, and so on. Or start a fund-raising drive in your office for such organizations.*

☆ *Bake a cherry pie and leave it on someone's doorstep.*

☆ *Slip a $20 bill into the pocketbook of a needy friend (or stranger).*

☆ Get a big piece of paper and a magic marker, and sit back to back with a friend. Across the top of the page, write the words physical, emotional, aesthetic, spiritual, and relational. Set an alarm clock for ten minutes and make a thank-you card for all the people, places, or things that have affected you in those dimensions. When the time is up, share your paper with one another.

☆ Organize your friends and workmates to gather their old clothes and give them to homeless people.

☆ Go to an AIDS hospice or hospital ward and see what you can do for one person.

☆ Next time you go over a toll bridge pay the toll for the car behind you and don't forget to thank the toll taker.

I was in Los Angeles visiting my father who was in the hospital. He had gone into a coma and my sister and I had gone there expecting to say good-bye to him. But he had revived.

It had been quite an ordeal emotionally, dealing with the hospital atmosphere with the thought my father was dying, and then the relief when he came out of the coma. As we were leaving the hospital, we had to cross a courtyard and this tiny little girl—she couldn't have been more than fifteen months old—came running over to me with a beautiful bouquet of pink and purple flowers in her hand. She held out her arm to show me the flowers. I bent down to smell them and she put them into my hand. When I took the flowers, she stepped back, got a huge smile on her face, and clapped her hands. It was like a gift from the angels.

"Let the beauty we love be what we do."
        -Rumi

It was one of those ice-cream days of summer. The kind where it gets so hot that you are almost literally pulled down to the ice-cream parlor. When I found myself there this particularly steamy day, it was an ice-cream zoo—people standing in a line that ran out the door, people standing around the front eating ice cream, people wandering down the street, ice cream in hand. After waiting patiently for what seemed like forever, I finally got my double scoop of strawberry (I never was all that adventurous about ice cream). As I turned to leave, I came across a small boy standing in the doorway with a empty sugar cone in his hand and two scoops of strawberry melting away on the sidewalk. He had giant tears streaming down his cheeks and his mother was saying, "You should have been more careful." I took one look at his double scoop of strawberry on the sidewalk and my double scoop still neatly packed into a sugar cone, handed it to him, and walked away.

had just
completed my training as
a chiropractor and I wanted to
open an office. Then the perfect
place just fell into my lap, but I did
not have any money. None. And I needed
not only rent money, but money for a table,
chairs, and so forth. I called a few friends but was
only able to raise around a thousand dollars total—not
nearly enough. Then I got a call from a man who was the
cook at the school where I had trained. He told me to
stop by because he had something for me. When I went
over, he led me into the back room of the kitchen. There
on a table was a large stack of money. Handing me a
piece of paper and a pen, he told me to count the money
and write up an IOU. It was around $6,000—an

*"He alone is great who turns the voice
of the wind into a song made sweeter by his own loving."*
        -Kahil Gibran

unbelievably trusting and
generous gift. After getting
my office set up and beginning my
practice, things suddenly started going
very badly. Within a few months nine friends
and relatives of mine died. Here I was trying to
build a practice at the same time that I was being
overwhelmed by grief and working under the added
pressure that it was someone else's money I was working
with. As a result the practice was not going well and I
was rapidly approaching bankruptcy.

One day I woke up, went into the office, and
decided that something good had to happen. So I gave
my secretary a raise. She said, "You can't afford to do
that," but I told her I couldn't afford not to. That day
everything began to turn around and I was eventually
able to pay back the cook.

"Let us be kinder to one another."
-Aldous Huxley, on his deathbed

An act of kindness
can sometimes take incredible
courage. I was at the county fair many
years ago with my mother. I remember
it was a very, very hot day and all around
us children and parents were melting down.
We were walking behind a woman with two
small children. The children were crying and
whining and the mother was getting increasingly
upset. Finally she started to scream at them to shut up;
then she turned around and struck them both very hard.
Just to see this happen right in front of me made me feel
like I had been hit as well.

Of course her kids starting crying even more and

"The best portions of a good man's life,
His little, nameless, unremembered acts,
Of kindness and love."
        -William Wordsworth

the mother was on the
verge of completely losing
control when my mother walked
up to her, touched her arm, and said
something like, "You poor dear, don't
worry, sometimes things just get out of
control for a moment." Then my mother
offered to take the children over to the ice-
cream stand, buy them some ice cream, and sit
with them while the woman took a little walk to
compose herself. She returned in about ten minutes,
thanked my mother, hugged her children, and went on.

*"Life is short and we have
never too much time for gladdening the hearts of those
who are travelling the dark journey with us. Oh be swift
to love, make haste to be kind."*
-Henri Frederick Amiel

$\mathcal{W}$e were on vacation in Florida, with four kids all under the age of ten. The weather had been very hot and humid so this particular day we decided to pack a cooler full of sandwiches and soft drinks and drive out along the coast until we found a nice beach. It was sort of an adventure since we really didn't know where we were going, but after a while we found a really beautiful beach that was pretty isolated. We parked and unloaded ourselves onto the sand. It was really great, except that, after a few hours, it just got too hot for the kids and they were starting to whine and complain. So we decided to head back to the air-conditioned hotel. When we got back to the car, however, there were the keys, dangling from the ignition with all the windows rolled up and all the doors locked. In frustration I screamed, "Who locked the doors?" to

"When strangers start acting like neighbors . . . communities are reinvigorated."
-Ralph Nader

which Beth, my five-year-old, responded, "You tell us always to lock the doors." I felt totally defeated.

At first I was just going to smash the window in, but after Beth's evenhanded comment, I thought that would be a bit too violent. So I walked up the road about a half mile to a house along the beach. When I got there, this elderly couple invited me in, let me use their telephone to call roadside service, then packed me into their car and drove back to pick up the rest of my family. They brought us all back to their home, and within a few minutes the kids were swimming in their pool while my wife and I sat on an air-conditioned veranda sipping a cool drink and swapping vacation stories. Roadside service came and went and three hours later we headed back to our hotel, much refreshed and glowing from the surprising and wonderful experience.

"It is better to give and receive."
-Bernard Gunther

One cold September day, a friend and I decided to eat lunch together downtown before heading back to our respective suburbs. As we made our way down the steps to the restaurant entrance, we spied a young mother off to one side, trying to corral the energy of her toddler in the middle of a tantrum. I was struck by the energy of the child's cry and the writhing movements of her body. The mother was struggling too, trying to give her daughter some space to vent safely without making too much of a spectacle. As the mother of a six-year-old myself, I could relate.

We walked on past, went into the restaurant, and were promptly seated. But the scene I had just witnessed would not leave my mind. I had barely sat down before I

"Do everything with a mind that lets go. Do not expect praise or reward."
-Achaan Chah

stood again, telling my friend that I was going to see what I could do for the mom. Stepping outside, I reached out my hand to touch the troubled mother's arm and asked, "Are you all right?" The young woman was clearly surprised. She was holding her somewhat-settled crying daughter on her lap and things had more or less run their course. "Do you have kids?" she asked. Then, as her daughter climbed up and down the stairs, we shared stories, frustrations, favorite ways to cope with our children's seemingly boundless energy. It was quite a few minutes into the conversation before we introduced ourselves and discovered to our amazement that we lived just four blocks from each other in the same small town.

"A knowledge of the path cannot be substituted for putting one foot in front of the other."
-M. C. Richards

A good friend
and I had finally gotten together
one evening after months of trying
to make our schedules and the fifty
miles separating us fit together somehow.
We went out to eat and as usual had a great
time talking about everything. I am always amazed at
how quickly and deeply we reconnect even after months
of barely speaking on the telephone.

While we were catching up on each other's lives,
she noticed a man sitting alone at a table in the corner of
the restaurant and commented to me that he looked sad,
as if he were lacking for company. When we had finished
our meal, I insisted on paying and my friend went along
smiling. When the waiter came to pick up the check, my
friend told him that she would like to pay—anonymously—for the dinner of the man in the corner.
I realized again why I cared about her so much.

*"No joy can equal
the joy of serving others."*
        -Sai Baba

$\mathcal{T}$his is a story that's about fifty years old. During World War II, my father-in-law and his pregnant wife, who were living in Texas, wanted to visit with his parents in Oklahoma before he went to the Philippines. They had to drive back roads all the way. To their dismay, they had a flat and no spare tire. Walking several deserted miles, they finally came to a farmhouse. Now this was in the days when rubber was rationed, but the farmer who lived there took off a tire from his car and said, "Drive into town, get your tire fixed, and leave mine at the gas station. I'll get my tire back later on." His trusting action really saved the day for my in-laws.

"I try to give to the poor people for love what the rich could get for money. No. I wouldn't touch a leper for a thousand pounds, yet I willingly cure him for the love of God."
                                        -Mother Teresa

Practice
Random Acts of Kindness!

☆ *If someone in your neighborhood leaves on a trip and forgets to stop the newspaper, pick them up and put them in a safe out-of-view spot.*

☆ *Next time you go to the movies, pick out someone behind you in the line and tell the ticket seller you want to pay for their ticket as well. Make sure to ask that they not reveal who paid for their ticket.*

☆ *If you have any artistic abilities, buy a shopping bag full of art supplies and take it and yourself out to a playground or recreation center in a poor neighborhood and go to it.*

☆ *If you know someone who is going through a bad day or a difficult time in life, make it better by doing something—anything—to let him or her know someone cares . . . and don't let on who did it!*

☆ *Laugh out loud often and share your smile generously.*

☆ *Praise the work or attitude of a person you work with to someone else in the office in a time, place, and manner that is outside of all office politics.*

☆ *If you are the boss, bring your secretary a cup of coffee in the morning.*

☆ *Buy gift certificates—for a kids' clothing store, a record store, whatever suits your mood—and find a way to get them—anonomously—to people you think could really use them.*

When I was in college, I worked part-time at a sporting goods store. There was a kid who would come by two or three times a week to visit with this baseball mitt that he wanted to buy. My manager and I would joke about him not only because he was so dedicated and persistent, but also because he had picked the best and most expensive mitt in the shop to get obsessed about.

This went on for months. The kid would come in, and you could tell he was so relieved that the mitt was still there. He would put it on, pound his fist into the pocket a couple of times, and then very carefully put it back onto the shelf and leave. Finally, one day he came

"Shall we make a new rule of life from tonight: always to try to be a little kinder than is necessary."
    -Sir James M. Barrie

in with a shoe box and a smile about eight miles wide and announced that he wanted to buy the mitt. So the manager brought the mitt over to the cash register while the kid counted out a shoe box worth of nickels, quarters, and dimes. His stash came to exactly $19.98. The mitt cost $79.98, not including tax. My manager looked at the price tag, and sure enough the 7 was a little smudged, enough that a desperately hopeful seven-year-old could imagine it to be a 1. Then he looked at me, smiled, and very carefully recounted. "Yep, exactly $19.98." Wrapping up the mitt, he gave it to the boy.

"T'was a thief said the last kind word to Christ. Christ took the kindness and forgave the theft."
-Robert Browning

*Y*ou hear stories
about tourists trying to drive in
San Francisco all the time. I discovered
a whole new twist one day when I was
walking up a particularly steep hill and saw
a car stopped near the top with a very frightened
woman inside. As I watched, she made a few attempts
to get moving but each time seemed to lose more ground
than she gained. Then a man came out of the corner
market. The next thing I know, she gets out of the car
and goes around to the passenger side while he climbs
into the driver's seat and promptly drives the car up over

*"Miracles occur naturally
as expressions of love. The real miracle is the love that
inspires them. In this sense everything that comes from
love is a miracle."*
         -A Course in Miracles

the top of the dreaded hill. By then, I had reached the store where the helpful man's wife was standing, watching the proceedings. She told me that her husband, who owns the market, has been doing that for years, and that during the summer-time—peak tourist season—he will "rescue" as many as ten scared drivers a week.

"Charity is in the heart of man, and righteousness in the path for men. Pity the man who has lost his path and does not follow it and who has lost his heart and does not know how to recover it. When people's dogs and chicks are lost they go out and look for them and yet the people who have lost their hearts do not go out and look for them. The principle of self-cultivation consists in nothing but trying to look for the lost heart."
-Mencius

*O*ne day when
I was a senior in high school,
I was walking home from school
and noticed an elderly couple standing
at the base of a very tall pine tree. They
were looking up and yelling and they were
obviously very upset. I thought that maybe their
cat had gotten stuck in the tree, and since I had spent
many of my best times as a young boy climbing trees, I
went to see if I could help.

At the top of the tree was a very young girl. She
couldn't have been more than three or four years old.
Apparently she was staying with her grandparents and,
when they weren't looking, had shimmied up the tree.
They had already called the fire department, but I felt

*"If you stop to be kind,
you must swerve often from your path."*
-Mary Webb

like I should at least climb
up far enough so that if she
started to fall I might be able
to catch her. When I got within a
few feet of the little girl, she gave me
this huge smile and said "Hi." I almost
started laughing because she was not at all
scared; in fact she looked as much at ease as a
monkey on its home branch. We ended up talking for a
while about how great it felt to climb trees, and as we
talked, cradled in that pine tree, I could feel my whole
body relaxing into the tree. I had this wonderful feeling
that everything was just right with the world.
Then she said, "We better go down now," and, as

*"Wherever there is a
human being there is an opportunity for kindness."*
-Seneca

we climbed down the tree
(I was very careful to keep
myself close and below her),
I could see that she was never
in any real danger. She moved
as though she could scramble up
and down that tree a million times
and never come close to slipping. As
I walked home, I realized that that was
the first time I had crawled out onto the
limb of a tree in many, many years. The thought
made me want to go back and thank that little girl.

"May it be, oh Lord,
That I seek not so much to be consoled
as to console, to be understood as to understand, to be
loved as to love. Because it is in giving oneself that one
receives; it is in forgetting oneself that one is found; it is
in pardoning that one obtains pardon."
　　　　-St. Francis of Assisi

112

When I was in high school, I had a friend who asked me to help him plant some weeping willow trees down by a creek. It seems that he had watched every year as the banks of this creek had been increasingly eaten away. It had gotten to the point where the water was threatening to overflow into the nearby housing development. My friend had obviously done his research; he found out that willows grew quickly, easily, and with a great spreading root system that drinks up lots of water which would stabilize the creek bank. When I met him at the creek, he had a huge bundle of willow branches in his arms. We spent most of the day planting these willow sprigs up and down the endangered curve.

Many years later, I was home visiting and found myself walking down by that creek. Where we spent that afternoon is now a beautiful idyllic bend with a long curving row of large graceful willows bending out over the water.

$\mathcal{F}$ebruary is not
my time of year. I don't know
if it is my own seasonal mood
swings or just that my surroundings
have such a big impact on me that after
so many months of winter, my mood begins
to resemble the dirty, slushy, grey world outside.
I begin to walk around as if a dark cloud were inside
my head. Everything looks gloomy and depressing.

A few years ago I was in the middle of a particularly depressing February and even though I had gone
through this feeling many times before and knew it
would eventually pass, I had gotten to the point where I
was beginning to believe it would never get better. It was
a Friday and my children were off to visit their father for
the weekend. I can remember thinking as I went to sleep
that night that this time I would be stuck forever in

*"There must be more
to life than having everything!"*
      -Maurice Sendak

winter. When I woke up there was an eerie silence all over the house. I walked over to the front door and opened it. Outside, the world had remade itself into the most sparkling, beautiful, and inviting place imaginable. A late-night snowstorm had covered everything with a soft pristine layer of white. The sun was up and shining brightly; everywhere I looked the snow was dancing with light. Suddenly all the dark clouds in my mind were gone and I started laughing. I must have looked like a crazy woman standing in my bathrobe at the front door, laughing out into the silent empty yard. It seemed like a great joke. Winter, the dark dreary tormentor of my soul, had pulled a fast one and slipped in a day of incredible purity and beauty just to remind me of the possibilities in life.

"Give help rather than advice."
-Luc de Vauvenargues

had just graduated
from college and had gone back to
the town I grew up in to visit friends.
My parents had sold the family home a
few years back and moved out of state so
I also took the opportunity to drive by the
old house just to see it. Out in the front yard,
perched in "my" giant oak tree, was a boy about
ten years old. I stopped the car, went over to introduce
myself, and told the boy that when I was his age I practi-
cally lived in that tree. He thought that was real funny
because he said his mother was always telling people
that he lives in that tree.

    While we were standing there talking, laughing,
and feeling very good about our shared tree, a car drove

"Let us not be
justices of the peace, but angels of peace."
       -St. Theresa of Lisieux

up to the curb right in front of us. A middle-aged man got out of the driver's side, came around to the passenger side, and helped a very frail-looking old man out of the car. I guess we were both staring, but the old man just walked right up to the tree, patted it on the side, looked at us, and said, "I planted this tree sixty years ago when there was nothing here but fields. I still like to come visit it now and then." Then he turned around, got back into the car, and drove away. We were both so shocked we didn't say a word until after the old man had left. Then the boy just looked at me and said, "Wow."

"No man giveth, but with intention of good to himself; because gift is voluntary, and of all voluntary acts the object is to every man his own good."
-Thomas Hobbes

117

I had no money.
I had made the heartbreaking
decision to end my marriage of
eight years and move out on my
own. A friend had offered me the
vacant bedroom in his apartment to
be my nest while I got on my feet again.
I had to be very selective about the things
I could use in this very small space. And there
wasn't just me to consider. My young son would
be staying with me several nights a week. So the queen-
sized bed I already owned was not a practical choice. I
began looking through the want ads for a used trundle

"The only gift is a
portion of thyself . . . the poet brings his poem; the
shepherd his lamb . . . the girl, a handkerchief of
her own sewing."
                    -Ralph Waldo Emerson

118

bed, so I could get two beds
for the space of one. Asking prices
ranged from $100 to $200 for the nice
ones. Cheaper ones seemed to be gone
by the time I picked up the phone.
One day I spoke to a good friend about my frustration and resignation about sleeping on the floor for a
while. It just so happened that a wooden trundle bed was
sitting on her front porch, a recent discard by one of the
neighboring tenants. I picked it up and my son and I
slept peacefully for months on it.

"Of neighborhoods,
benevolence is the most beautiful. How can
the man be considered wise who when he had the choice
does not settle in benevolence."
-Confucius

was out to dinner
with a friend and we ended up
talking for a while with our waitress.
She was one of those waitresses who
was such a pleasure she made the whole
dining experience that much more enjoyable.
She told us about how she was working two jobs
and trying to put herself through school at night.

It was not a very expensive restaurant, and I think
our total bill was less than $20. But when we paid, we left
her a $100 tip. What a great feeling.

*"The great, dominant,
all controlling fact of this life is the innate bias of the
human spirit, not towards evil, as the theologists tell us,
but towards good. But for that bias, man would never
have been man; he would only have been one more species
of wild animal ranging a savage, uncultivated globe, the
reeking battleground of sheer instinct and appetite."*
-William Archer

$\mathcal{T}$here was a time in my life when everything was working so smoothly, I found myself sitting at home one Saturday with all my work done, all my household chores completed: dishes washed, laundry folded and put away, house dusted, grocery shopping completed, and that delicious feeling of having nothing to do. Then I thought about a friend from work who was a single mother of two small children and never seemed to have the time for anything. I jumped into my car, drove over to her house, walked, in and said, "Put me to work." At first she didn't really believe it, but we ended up having a great time, cleaning like mad, taking time out to feed and play with the kids, and then diving back into the chores.

"Charity is the bone shared with the dog when you are just as hungry as the dog."
-Jack London

flew into
O'Hare Airport and had a
two-hour layover before my
connecting flight. So I went to
the first bar I could find, ordered
a drink, opened my book, and proceeded
to wait out the time. Somewhere around the
halfway point, I pulled out my ticket to double-
check the time of departure and flight number. The
gate I was leaving from was almost at the opposite end of
the airport, so I left what I thought was plenty enough
time to get there and check in. By the time I made it all
the way over to the right gate I was almost the last person in line to board. That's when I realized my ticket was
missing. There I was, checking every pocket, emptying

*"The course of human
history is determined, not by what happens in the skies,
but by what takes place in our hearts."*
        -Sir Arthur Keith

the contents of my briefcase,
rechecking my pockets, and all
the time I had this sick feeling in
my stomach that I had left the ticket
on the table in the cocktail lounge
at the other end of the airport. Just as
I was about to go into a major panic, a man
comes running up to the gate and says, "I found this
ticket on a chair in the bar. When I saw what flight it was
for, I figured maybe I could catch you in time." I barely
had time to thank him before I was rushed onto the plane
and the doors closed.

*"The ideals which have
lighted my way, and time after
time have given me new courage to face life cheerfully,
have been Kindness, Beauty, and Truth . . . . The trite
subjects of human efforts—possessions, outward success,
luxury—have always seemed to me contemptible."*
-Albert Einstein

$\mathcal{I}$ was standing
in line getting ready to board a
plane when this guy comes rushing
up to the ticket counter. He had obviously
been running like O. J. Simpson through the
terminal and was furious when the woman at
the counter told him his reservation had been
cleared and his seat given away. She offered to get
him a confirmed seat on the next flight, which unfortunately was not leaving for nearly five hours, but he
would have none of it. He started screaming about how
important it was that he get to Chicago by seven, how
irresponsible the airline was when, after all, he had a
confirmed ticket, how he wanted to see the supervisor,
and on and on and on.

*"Kindness is a language
which the dumb can speak, the deaf can understand."*
                                        -C. N. Bovee

124

Finally he stopped his tirade and, in a very quite voice, said, "I'm really sorry. I'm just completely stressed out and I can't believe I am going to miss this meeting." Right then an old man, who had been standing in front of me in the boarding line watching this whole thing, stepped up to the counter and said, "Here, take my seat. I'm retired and I'm in no real hurry to get anywhere." The guy was so happy and so ashamed at the same time it looked like he was going to cry. Then he took the ticket and got on the plane.

"Man should not consider his material possessions his own, but common to all, so as to share them without hesitation when others are in need."
-St. Thomas Aquinas

grew up in
what we would now call
a dysfunctional family. My
parents materially were quite
well off, but we lived amidst
emotional chaos and confusion in
a wealthy suburb of Philadelphia. As
with most children, I simply assumed that
this was the way it was and that the problems,
the undercurrents of anger and hostility, were somehow
my fault. One day when I was still very young, after a
particularly painful and confusing series of interactions
with my parents, our maid took me aside to talk to me.
She told me that she did not care if it cost her her job, she
just could not continue to be a silent observer. She told

*"A gift consists not in
what is done or given, but in the intention
of the giver or doer."*
    -Seneca

me that my parents were
crazy, that they were acting
very badly, and not at all like
good loving parents should act
toward their children. She told me
that I was a good, sweet girl and that the
situation was not my fault. It must have taken a
lot of courage for her to do that. Not only to overcome
the natural hesitation to intervene between parents and
children, but to take the risk that I would not say something about our talk to my parents. I never did talk about
it. It was an incredible gift. Her words gave me the expla-
nation I needed, a way to stop blaming everything on
myself.

*"Five things constitute
perfect virtue: gravity, magnanimity,
earnestness, sincerity and kindness."*
-Confucius

*O*ne Friday afternoon I was on my way to set up for a book fair in San Francisco. Waiting at a stoplight in front of the convention center, I noticed a handicapped woman on the street corner. She was sitting against a fence, a walker by her side, surrounded by what was probably all of her belongings. As I watched, another woman, perfectly coiffed, in high heels and a power suit, came up to her with a bag. Without a word, the businesswoman proceeded to lay out prepared food, which she had obviously bought "to go," around the street person so that she could easily reach the food from a sitting position. The homeless woman looked on in grateful

*"Kindness
is the noblest weapon to conquer with."
        -American proverb*

amazement, as if her guardian angel had appeared out of nowhere just in time. In fact, she had. Three days later, when I was leaving the convention center, I passed the same woman leaning against the same fence. This time, a man in a van was at the stoplight, honking and holding money out to the woman. She was trying to move, but couldn't get up. Quickly, I ran to the van, grabbed the money, and brought it to her. I felt so happy to see people taking care of this woman, and pleased that my weekend was bracketed by tokens of generosity.

"There is a Law that man should love his neighbor as himself. In a few hundred years it should be as natural to mankind as breathing or the upright gait; but if he does not learn it he must perish."
-Alfred Adler

129

$\mathcal{M}$y girlfriend and
I are avid backpackers. I can't even
describe the feeling I get after we lock
up the car and hit the trail, and every step
is one step farther into the hills and one step
farther away from all the crazy stuff that goes
on in the world. In my mind it is such a different
reality once we are on the trail, and I guess that is why I
always put all my "worldly" things in a small green zip-
up bag and stuff it away in a corner of my backpack. I
mean everything—my wallet, with all my ID, credit
cards, license, etc., all my money, my keys—everything
you need to survive in the modern world and everything
that is irrelevant back in the woods.

    This particular trip was a five-day trek through

*"By the accident of
fortune a man may rule the
world for a time, but by virtue of love and kindness he
may rule the world forever."*
    -Lao-Tse

some of the most beautiful
parts of the Cascades. As we
headed back down toward the
parking area where we had left the
car, I was really sad to be leaving what to
me was such a simple and beautiful way of
living. I could just feel the tension and anxiety
beginning to creep back into my body as we got
closer and closer to civilization. When we finally got to
the car there was a small piece of paper tucked under the
windshield-wiper blade that read, "left rear tire." I
walked back and looked at the left rear tire but it was
fine. The note made no sense to me at all—three seconds
back into the world and

*"I feel no need for any other
faith than my faith in the kindness of human beings . . . I
am so absorbed in the wonder of earth and the life upon it
that I cannot think of heaven and angels."*
-Pearl S. Buck

131

already lunacy. Then I
started fishing through my
backpack for my green bag. It
wasn't there. I looked back at the
left rear tire—there was the bag. I have
no idea when I lost it, I have no idea who
found it, or how they ever found my car amid
all the possible parking places in that part of the
Cascades. My keys, my wallet, nearly $100 in cash, all
neatly tucked in my zip-up green bag sitting on top of
my left rear tire. Thank you, whoever you are, you gave
me back much more than you know.

*"Kindness makes the
difference between passion and caring. Kindness is tenderness, kindness is love, perhaps greater than love . . . kindness is goodwill, kindness says "I want you to be happy."
Kindness comes very close to the benevolence of God."*
        -Randolph Ray

have been going to the same bagel/coffee shop every Sunday for years. One morning in the middle of a great dreary drizzly weekend, I trudged in dripping wet with my newspaper carefully tucked under my overcoat and ordered my usual bagel with lox and cream cheese and an expresso. I was casually informed that my coffee had already been paid for. I looked around expecting to see some friend sitting somewhere but didn't, and when I asked, the young woman at the register just smiled and said someone paid for twenty coffees and you are number eight. I sat there for almost an hour, reading my paper, and watching more surprised people come in to find their morning coffee pre-paid. There we all were, furtively at first and then with big funny smiles on our faces, looking at everyone else in the restaurant trying to figure out who had done this incredible thing, but mostly just enjoying the experience as a group. It was a beautiful blast of sunshine on an otherwise overcast winter day.

133

Practice
Random Acts of Kindness!

☆ *Take the opportunity in conversations with friends to tell them about kindnesses you have experienced and ask about their experiences. Just talking about acts of kindness brings them alive in the world.*

☆ *Get your children to go through their toys and put aside those they want to donate to children who are less fortunate.*

☆ *Buy a giant box of candy at the theatre, take one and pass it down the row to share.*

☆ *Next time you go to the ice-cream parlor, pay for a few free cones to be given to the next kids to come in.*

☆ If you have an infirmed person living near you, offer to do the grocery shopping for him or her.

☆ Pick up the mail for a senior or someone else who could use the assistance.

☆ Send a fax to someone you don't know and start a random acts of kindness chain fax letter.

☆ If there is a garden you pass frequently and enjoy, stop by one day and leave a note letting the occupants know how much pleasure their garden gives you.

☆ Make a dedication on your local radio station to all those people who smiled at strangers today.

A friend of mine
was going back East to college.
Not only was it her first time away
from home but, even more overwhelming
to a California baby, it was going to be her
first true winter. She spent many months looking
for the perfect winter coat, a task all the more difficult
when even long pants seemed stifling. Finally, two days
before her departure, she found the coat that would keep
her from getting frostbite and maybe even homesick.
Unfortunately, the store didn't have the size she needed,
although one of their other locations thirty miles away
did. In desperation, she told the saleswoman her

"The government in
which I believe is that which is based on mere
moral sanction . . . the real law lives in the kindness of our
hearts. If our hearts are empty, no law or political reform
can fill them."
      -Leo Tolstoy

situation, who then proceeded to console her by promising that she would "take care of it." Two days and a few logistical phone calls later, the saleswoman met my friend at the airport gate, perfect-fitting coat in hand. The saleswoman was definitely acting above and beyond the call of duty, since I'm sure her job description didn't require her to deal with airport parking.

"Believe nothing, O monks, merely because you have been told it . . . Do not believe what your teacher tells you merely out of respect for the teacher. But whatsoever, after due examination and analysis, you find to be kind, conducive to the good, the benefit, the welfare of all beings—that doctrine believe and cling to, and take it as your guide."
-Buddha

137

*W*e recently had
the traumatic experience of having
our house burn down, followed by
the equally unsettling experience of trying
to deal with the insurance company. How do
you prove what you lost when it is completely
and totally gone?

Our home was built over fifty years ago and,
surprisingly, the city still had original blueprints on file.
This proved at first to be more of a problem than a help,
because we had completely remodeled five years before
it burned, adding on an entirely new floor, extending the
house out in the backyard, and building a real garage to
replace the tiny box common to homes built in the thir-
ties. Needless to say, the insurance company

"All things whatsoever
ye would that men should do to you, do ye even so to
them: for this is the law of the Prophets."
        -Matthew 7:12

generously offered to
replace the house as specified
on the original blueprints. We of
course had had a drawer full of pictures
showing the remodeling job, but that drawer
was gone along with everything else. Other than
our word and that of friends and neighbors, we
had no proof of what we had lost.
Our problem was mentioned in a paragraph in the
local newspaper, and a few days later we received a
photo album in the mail filled with pictures of our house!
A man who had been an architecture student at the time
we remodeled our home had done a project on upgrad-
ing instead of destroying housing stock and, unbe-
knownst to us, had used our house as a visual example.

*"He that is kind is free, though
he is a slave; he that is evil is a slave, though he be a king."*
-St. Augustine

He had done a complete
photo history: before, during,
and after. In his letter, his told us
that it had all be quite accidental—that
the very day he started looking for a project
was the first day our contractor showed up to
start working. He had approached him to find
out what they were going to do, and our contractor
had been very cooperative, showing him all the plans
and promising to show him all the gritty details as he
progressed. When we showed our insurance adjuster the
photos, we could see him gulp—and they ended up
paying even more than we had expected.

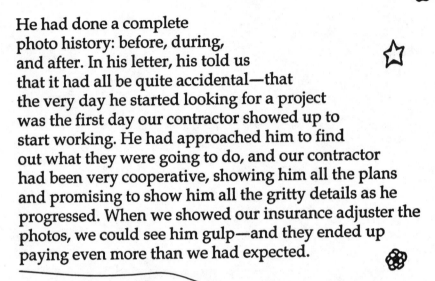

"Compassionate the mountains rise
Dim with the wistful dimness of old eyes
That, having looked on life time out of mind,
Know that the simple gift of being kind
Is greater than all wisdom of the wise."
        -DuBose Heyward

ride the bus to and from work every day—it's about a thirty-five-minute trip. When you commute like I do, you have a real appreciation for the difference between sitting down, which allows you to either doze off or read and just relax, and standing up, during which you are constantly being tossed to one side or another, trying not to smash into other standees and constantly moving out of the way so people can get on or off. It makes you develop a keen sense of strategy for getting a seat. I've discovered that if I cut across the hill a few blocks to catch the bus earlier in its route, it greatly increases my odds of finding a seat. There is one elderly woman who is pretty much on the same schedule as I am and before my discovery I used to

"What wisdom can you find that is greater than kindness?"
-Jean Jacques Rousseau

get on the bus and she would
already be there—usually seated
while I remained standing. After my
discovery, she would get on the bus and
sometimes end up standing while I was already
seated. It made me feel a little odd, like I had somehow
cheated her, but I did not give up my seat.

One day coming back from work I was standing
when I was suddenly hit by this wave of nausea. It felt
like I was going to pass out, but I was trying very hard
not to make a scene. Suddenly I felt a hand on my arm

*"I believe that man
will not merely endure; he will prevail. He is immortal,
not because he alone among the creatures has an inexhaustible voice, but because he has a soul, a spirit capable
of kindness and compassion."*
        -William Faulkner

guiding me down into a seat.
It was the woman from my morning
bus whom I almost never saw going back.
Very gently she helped me into what had been her
seat and then hovered over me in a wonderfully protec-
tive way to give me some privacy to disappear in. By the
time we got back to our neighborhood, I felt well enough
to thank her and get home.
Ever since that day, I *always* give her my seat in the
morning; in fact, I look forward to it.

*"We may have all come
on different ships, but we're in the same boat now."*
-Martin Luther King, Jr.

For many years,
our next-door neighbor was this
very sweet and unusual old woman.
Her husband had died quite young and
she had lived alone ever since her children
grew up and moved out. When my brother
and I were young, she always treated us as real
people, not just a couple of kids. She would talk to
us seriously about what was happening in our lives,
and actually took an interest in things like the wins and
losses of our baseball teams. She also had what at the
time was a really hot car—a silver 1957 Chevy—that she
took great care of. As she got older, her son took over the
duties of occasionally washing and polishing the car, but
then he moved out of state.

"Our brightest blazes of gladness are commonly kindled by unexpected sparks."
        -Dr. Johnson

One day my brother and I were at our parents' house for Thanksgiving dinner and we noticed that her poor old Chevy was looking very sad. Later that night we snuck into her driveway, washed the car inside and out, waxed it, and polished all the chrome; when we were done it was shining just like a floor model.

That was nearly five years ago, and since then we have made regular guerrilla raids into her driveway. I don't think she knows who is doing it, but my mother reports that she has taken to going "cruising" in her car, and always laughs and tells my mother she has an "automotive angel."

"I keep my ideals, because in spite of everything I still believe that people are really good at heart."
-Anne Frank

Several months ago,
I found myself driving in Los Angeles
through morning rush hour traffic.
Traffic was heavy, but everyone was going
quite fast. Suddenly a white Mazda RX7 in
the slow lane spun out, doing four complete
circles across the freeway. I stared in disbelief
as cars swerved to avoid the whirling white dervish.
By some miracle, all the traffic missed the car, which
came to rest on the opposite side of the freeway, in the
fast lane, facing the wrong way. No one stopped; everyone continued on as though nothing had happened.

I pulled off the freeway, got out of my car, walked
to the Mazda, opened the door, and pulled out a sobbing,
semihysterical woman who kept saying, "Did you see
what they did? They ran me off the road." I put my arms
around the woman, who collapsed into them and sobbed

"When I give I give myself."
      -*Walt Whitman*

as though her heart would break.
She finally calmed down enough to
explain that a blue Bronco had forced her
off the road, causing her car to spin out. There
we stood—two women, total strangers, holding and
comforting one another on a busy freeway.
Suddenly a third car, a blue Bronco, stopped. A
third woman jumped out, also crying. She ran over to the
woman in my arms, saying over and over again, "I am so
sorry; I didn't see you; please forgive me." The first
woman turned from me to the newcomer, and they
melted into a sobbing embrace of "please forgive me's"
and "it's OK's." When both women had calmed down,
we figured out how to get the Mazda turned in the right
direction, and, once accomplished, jumped back in our
own cars and went on our way.

"T'was her thinking of others that made you think of her."
-Elizabeth Browning

Thoughts
on
Random
Acts
of
Kindness

I don't like this *random* word. I can understand the reframing of the notion of random violence, but for me, even random kindness triggers a similar shrug of my shoulders, a feeling of powerlessness. I hate the word. I've taken to calling it the *r-word.*

I'm not interested in ideas that seem to encourage the notion of being a passive agent. And while I acknowledge that sometimes life is painful and difficult, I also don't subscribe to "shit happens." *Random* is the kind of adjective that goes with a verb like *happens*—no actor, only the acted upon.

For a few years now I've been learning to bring more consciousness to my living, to pay attention to patterns, to use the ones that support me in new ways, to change the ones that don't. It's helping me to live more deeply, to find the intention beneath my intention.

150

My exploration has included reading such physicists as David Bohm. He is helping me to see how the universe is a living organism with an intricate pattern. When the universe makes sense to us, he calls those patterns the unfolded or explicate order. Those aspects that we have yet to name or unravel, or even fathom, he calls enfolded. It reminds me of encoded, and it feels to me like "random" events occur as a part of these still-enfolded patterns. Psychologist Stan Grof wrote in his book *The Holotropic Mind* that believing in a random universe is like thinking that a tornado could blow through a junkyard and assemble a 747 from the parts it found there. I liked that when I read it; it gave me a kind of "so there" feeling about the r-word.

But this isn't an intellectual argument for me, and name-dropping two brilliant people hasn't done anything to reduce the powerful visceral feelings I have about this word. That's because at bottom I believe that the universe is alive and mysterious, ultimately benevolent and orderly.

So I wrestle with "random" kindness, and try to imagine that it means those blessings that seem to appear around me without any effort on my part. Then I feel grateful for being able to take in the beauty or the love that surrounds me. That feels like a grace—my ability to really take in a kindness is as miraculous as the kindness itself. And I don't believe it's random.

I know that I have been the fortunate indirect object of much generosity—songs, sculptures, great and funny stories. I know they were not created with me in mind. But they were created or discovered, and then shared with intention.

I love intention, and consciousness, and discovery, and synchronicity. I am in awe of the creative mind at play in the creative universe. I believe in the magic of the unconscious mind, and when mine sends a message to my awareness, that's the universe revealing itself to me, that's God and me dancing. That's joy and mystery. That's not random.

andom acts of kindness. It has such a beautiful ring to it. A part of the beauty is undoubtedly the turnaround from that ugliest and most frightening of all phrases: random acts of violence. We all know of, or at least we know the deep personal fear of, random acts of violence. Haven't we all considered at some point that anytime, from anywhere, it could come, and for no apparent reason we—or someone we love—could be struck down? It's so easy to fear. It's so easy to create an almost palpable reality out of our imagined terror. Random acts of kindness ring pure and true as an antidote to that fear, as life-confirming revolutionary acts.

The word *kind* itself offers us so much insight: the *Oxford English Dictionary* begins its unraveling of the word *kind* by defining it as "the place or property, the character or quality derived from birth or native constitution. We are of that `kind'—to act according to one's nature; to do what is natural to one; by nature, naturally, the natural state, form or condition; the manner or way natural or proper to anyone."

Is not one of the great gifts of any act of kindness that it "brings us back," that it makes us feel that we have somehow returned to a place, to a feeling, that is somehow permanent, deeply rooted, and unchanging even as we begin once again to drift away? Kindness is at the heart of our belief that people are basically good. Kindness is the vehicle for all our hope that in the larger struggle between good and evil, good will prevail because ultimately we will return to kindness. It is our natural condition, our instinctual impulse to extend a hand.

And every hand we extend, every act of kindness we commit, sends a ripple out into the world that is magnified by every life it encounters. Fear and its real-world manifestation—violence—is stark and dramatic. It can temporarily consume, take over, and crowd out everything else.

Kindness is soft and subtle. It permeates everything it comes in contact with, remains as a permanent reminder of what could and should be.

What about acts of kindness toward ourselves? OK, so they're not random, but for a lot of people they are probably more difficult to do, much harder to remember, and maybe even more important in the long run. A friend of mine calls doing such things the new frontier. I like to think of them as refilling the cup. Kindness cannot flow from an empty cup, and the complex web of interactions we all seem to be caught up in these days almost demands that we empty everything we have and then some on a constant basis. So it is crucial that we refuel our own spirits so that we will want to be compassionate to others.

It's not an easy thing to do. Our jobs demand our time and energy because that part of us is bought and paid for. Then for many of us, our jobs ask even more— that we take them home, worry about them, and use up our precious resources of time, energy, and focus, all the while putting our own needs, our own desires, the things we want to do, farther and farther on the back burner.

Then comes the family. Kids, spouses, parents, siblings all make demands on us, both specific and general. Please pick up the pictures, drop off the dry cleaning, take me to soccer practice, call the insurance guy for me, check on this or that, do the grocery shopping, make sure the laundry is done, buy me some new socks . . . the list never ends. And for many people, particularly those sweet, loving, generous souls who usually end up carrying such a list, the doing for others not only never stops, but actually escalates as the "others" get more and more used to it and take it more and more for granted.

So what starts out as generous acts of kindness can gradually become hollow acts of servitude. The giver is doubly impoverished, because the acts themselves are no longer gifts but rather expected routines and because the burden of the obligations precludes the possibility of giving to oneself. In this way, those nonrandom acts of kindness toward friends, family, and lovers—the ones we all tend to assume come so easily and flow so freely— can actually prove to be not only the most difficult to maintain in the pure spirit of kindness, but can in fact turn so easily into vehicles of barter and bonds of obligation. Think hard about all the people in your life, about times when you received some gift of generosity from them that penetrated your heart and resonated with a clear, pure feeling of kindness. When was the last time one of your acts of kindness toward someone within your circle was clearly received in that way? If we are truthful, for most of us the answer is that it occurs all too infrequently, and the saddest part is that for all we do for each other, we have managed to reduce it from the magical realm of gifts freely and generously given to that of barter and obligation—currency and duties tallied up and traded back and forth.

No doubt there are many reasons why we fall into this sad pattern. But I believe that at the root of the problem is the saddest fact of all—that we take such poor care of our own needs and desires, that we all end up in a constant state of not having enough, not getting what we need, and wanting, always wanting, and expecting someone else to provide it.

For random acts of kindness to flourish we need

to begin in the hardest of all places, our own hearts. To reap a bountiful harvest of random acts of kindness, we need to begin by simple acts of kindness toward ourselves. Then we can truly give from overflow, from a heart brimming with loving kindness.

Join the Kindness Movement...

★ *Random Acts of Kindness Week*

is celebrated annually in February during the week of Valentine's Day.

Conari Press is interested in promoting the cause of kindness wherever and however we can. To that end, we are sponsoring *Random Acts of Kindness Week* with our nonprofit sponsor VOLUNTEERS OF AMERICA.

For more information on getting involved, please contact us:

Random Acts of Kindness Week
Conari Press
2550 Ninth Street, Suite 101
Berkeley, CA 94710

800-685-9595

Fax 510-649-7190

CONARI PRESS